*A Short
New Testament Syntax*

A Short
New Testament Syntax

Handbook with Exercises

Mark Andrew Brighton

WIPF & STOCK · Eugene, Oregon

A SHORT NEW TESTAMENT SYNTAX
Handbook with Exercises

Copyright © 2018 Mark Andrew Brighton. All rights reserved. Except for brief quotations in critical publications or reviews, no part of this book may be reproduced in any manner without prior written permission from the publisher. Write: Permissions, Wipf and Stock Publishers, 199 W. 8th Ave., Suite 3, Eugene, OR 97401.

Wipf & Stock
An Imprint of Wipf and Stock Publishers
199 W. 8th Ave., Suite 3
Eugene, OR 97401

www.wipfandstock.com

PAPERBACK ISBN: 978-1-5326-4555-6
HARDCOVER ISBN: 978-1-5326-4556-3
EBOOK ISBN: 978-1-5326-4557-0

Manufactured in the U.S.A.

Contents

Preface | ix

1. Grammatical Terminology | 1
2. Noun Cases | 24
   A. Vocative | 24
   B. Nominative | 24
   C. Genitive | 25
   D. Dative | 28
   E. Accusative | 30
3. Syntax of the Greek Article | 33
   A. Articles with Nouns | 33
   B. Articles as Pronouns | 34
   C. Articles as Substantives | 35
   D. Articles as Syntactical Markers | 35
4. Tenses of the Verb | 38
   A. Tense Aspect | 38
   B. Tenses in the Indicative | 39
   C. Tenses in Indirect Statements | 44
5. Voices of the Verb | 46
   A. Active Voice | 46
   B. Middle Voice | 46
   C. Passive Voice | 47
   D. Middle Only Verbs (Deponent) | 48

6. Indicative Mood | 49
   A. Independent Clauses | 49
   B. Conditional Statements | 50
   C. With ὅτι | 51

7. Subjunctive Mood | 53
   A. Hortatory | 53
   B. Deliberative | 53
   C. Prohibitions | 54
   D. ἵνα Plus Subjunctive | 54
   E. Future More Vivid Constructions | 56
   F. Present General Constructions | 56
   G. Fear Clauses | 57

8. Optative Mood | 58
   A. Wishes | 58
   B. Potential | 59
   C. Future Less Vivid Formulas | 59
   D. Dependent Clauses in Secondary Sequence | 59

9. Infinitive | 61
   A. Without the Article | 61
   B. With the Article | 64
   C. Prepositions with the Articular Infinitive | 65

10. Imperatives and Prohibitions | 67
    A. Direct Command | 67
    B. Entreaty | 67
    C. Prohibitions | 68

11. Participles | 69
    A. Attributive | 69
    B. Predicate | 70
    C. Supplementary | 70
    D. Noun Clause | 71
    E. Genitive Absolute | 71
    F. Tenses of the Participle | 71

Contents

12. Conditional Statements | 73
    A. Simple Conditions (First Class Conditions) | 73
    B. Future More Vivid (Third Class Conditions) | 74
    C. Future Less Vivid (Fourth Class Conditions) | 74
    D. Present General (Third Class Conditions) | 74
    E. Present Contrary to Fact (Second Class Conditions) | 74
    F. Past Contrary to Fact (Second Class Conditions) | 75

13. Uses of οὐ and μή | 76
    A. General Usage | 76
    B. Double Negatives | 76
    C. In Questions | 76
    D. Emphatic Negative | 77

14. Aramaic Constructions | 78
    A. καὶ ἐγένετο (ἐγένετο δέ) | 78
    B. καί | 79
    C. ἰδού | 79

15. Translation and Composition Exercises | 81
    Grammar Review: Emphasizing the Present Indicative | 81
    Grammar Review: Emphasizing the Imperfect and Aorist Indicative | 85
    Grammar Review: Emphasizing Strong Verbs | 88
    Noun Cases | 91
    Verb Tenses and Voices | 94
    Subjunctive | 97
    Participles | 101
    Infinitive | 105
    Conditional Statements | 109

Appendix: English to Greek Dictionary | 113

Preface

This handbook is designed primarily for second year students of New Testament Greek. Indeed, it was while teaching such classes that I first began writing it. There are many worthy books on New Testament syntax, but I became aware that second year students benefited most from clear and concise summaries. I have designed this handbook to fill such needs. Those who wish to explore these matters more deeply are encouraged to consult larger reference works.

This book's focus is upon basic syntax. Accordingly, I have included sections on grammatical terminology and translation exercises, which are designed to reinforce the explanations on syntax. In keeping with the book's focus, I have not included tables of grammar and would encourage students to consult their first year textbooks, when necessary, to relearn basic conjugations, declensions, and principle parts of verbs.

Lastly, I would like to dedicate this book to Robert Holst, a brilliant and humble scholar and a dear mentor who introduced the New Testament in Greek to me. I first came to love the language and literature as I sat in his classes long ago.

1

Grammatical Terminology

Abstract Noun

An abstract noun refers to a concept. "Love, joy, peace." (See Noun)

Accusative Case

One of the five cases in Greek. A noun in the accusative case often functions as the direct object in a sentence. (See Case and Direct Object)

Example: The performer sang them a *song*.

Example: I gave the child a *piece* of cake.

Active Voice

This term describes when the subject is acting upon something and contrasts to the passive voice, when the subject is being acted upon. (See Voice)

Example: The boy throws a ball. (Active voice)

Example: The boy is being thrown into the pool. (Passive voice)

Adjective

A word which modifies or further describes a noun or pronoun. These are words such as quick, high, heavy, wide, etc. An *attributive* adjective is joined to a noun or pronoun to make a phrase.

> Examples: The *quick* horse. The *deep* sea.

A *predicate* adjective is joined to a noun or pronoun by the verb "be" to make a sentence.

> Examples: He is *tall*. The ships are *beautiful*.

Adjectives can also be used independently as if they were nouns. In this case they are called *substantival* adjectives.

> Example: The land of the *free* and the home of the *brave*.

Adverb

A word which generally modifies or further describes a verb. Some adverbs, like "very" or "extremely," can modify other adjectives or adverbs.

> Examples: quietly, well, sadly, etc. I sing hymns *loudly*, but I do not sing them *very well*.

Agent

In a passive sentence, the doer of the action is called the agent. In English the agent is generally introduced with the word "by."

> Example: The ball was thrown *by the boy*.

In this example, the subject of the sentence, ball, is joined with a passive verb. The actual doer of the verb, the agent, is the boy.

Agreement

The formal correspondence of words in a sentence. Subjects will agree with their verbs.

> Example: *I am* a citizen of this country. *You are* a citizen of this country. *He is* a citizen of this country.

Pronouns will agree with their nouns.

> Examples: I saw the *cattle* in the field. *They* were eating grass.

> Examples: I spoke to the *mayor* yesterday. *She* was sitting in *her* office.

Besides subject-verb agreement and noun-pronoun agreement, in Greek, articles, adjectives, and participles generally will agree with their respective nouns or pronouns in number, gender, and case.

Antecedent

Antecedent literally means "going before." This term is applied to the noun to which a pronoun refers. The noun is called the antecedent because it generally (but not always) comes before the pronoun.

> Example: I saw *birds* flying in the sky yesterday. *They* were lovely. (The antecedent for the pronoun "they" is "birds.")

> Example: I gave the books to the *students, who* then read them carefully. (The antecedent of the relative pronoun "who" is "students.")

> Example: After *he* hit the baseball, the *boy* ran to first base. (The antecedent of "he" is "boy." Here is a case of a pronoun occurring before its antecedent.)

Apposition

When nouns are placed next to each other and describe the same person, place, or thing, they are said to be in apposition to each other.

> Example: *Paul*, an *apostle* of Christ Jesus, traveled around the Mediterranean world.

Article

An article is an adjective that defines the specificity of a noun. There are two types of articles in English: a definite article "the" and the indefinite article "a/an."

> Examples: the boy, a boy, the churches

Attributive Position

The attributive position describes how an adjective or other modifier such as a prepositional phrase is joined to a noun or pronoun to make a phrase. (See Adjective and Preposition)

> Examples: The *quick* horse. The man *in the house*.

Case

For English this term applies to nouns and pronouns. For Greek the term applies to articles, adjectives, and participles as well. The term describes how a noun or pronoun functions in a sentence. English has three cases; nominative, possessive, and objective. The objective case is commonly further divided into the indirect object and the direct object. Below we follow the terms for Greek grammars: vocative, nominative, genitive, dative, accusative.

- *Vocative*: Here a noun identifies the person or thing addressed.

    Example: *Professor*, can you explain this concept to me?

    Example: *Lord*, please have mercy upon me!

Grammatical Terminology

- *Nominative*: Here a noun or pronoun functions as the subject of a verb.

    Example: *I* gave my book to the student.

    Example: The *professor* gave the student's book to a classmate.

- *Genitive*: A genitive noun will express ownership or will in some way limit or further define the noun to which it is joined. It is often identified as a noun with an apostrophe or as a noun preceded by the word "of."

    Example: The professor gave the *student's* book to a classmate.

    Example: One can find *men's* shoes in a department store.

    Example: I gave the child a piece *of cake*.

- *Dative*: Here a noun is used as the indirect object in a sentence. (See Indirect Object) A noun in the dative case may have the word "to" or "for" preceding it.

    Example: The performer sang *them* a song. (The performer sang a song *for them*.)

    Example: I gave the *child* a piece of cake. (I gave a piece of cake *to the child*.)

- *Accusative*: Here a noun is used as the direct object in a sentence. (See Direct Object)

    Example: The performer sang them a *song*.

    Example: I gave the child a *piece* of cake.

Clause

A clause is a combination of a subject and predicate (see Predicate). When a clause expresses a complete idea, it is said to be an *independent clause*. But when a clause is incomplete unless joined to another clause, then it is called a *dependent* or *subordinate clause*. Note the following example:

 "When the laborers in the vineyard completed their work, the master gave the workers their pay."

This sentence has two clauses (two combinations of subject and predicate). The first clause, *"When the laborers in the vineyard completed their work,"* is an incomplete thought and is therefore the *subordinate* or *dependent clause*. The second clause, *"the master gave the workers their pay,"* is itself a complete idea and is therefore the *independent clause*. When two or more independent clauses are joined together, they constitute a *compound sentence*. When an independent clause is joined to one or more dependent clauses, they constitute a *complex sentence*.

> Example of a compound sentence: I drove my car to a dealer the other day, and the dealer sent it to the garage for repair.
>
> Example of a complex sentence: After I drove my care to the dealer the other day, the dealer sent it to the garage for repair.

Finally, when a clause takes the place of a noun, such as a direct object, it is called a *noun clause*. These will typically follow verbs of saying, thinking, believing, seeing, hearing, etc.

> Example: I see the teacher. (Here teacher is the direct object.) I see that the teacher is walking to class. (Here an entire clause functions as a direct object and is therefore called a noun clause.)

Collective Noun

A collective noun is a person, place, or thing that refers to group. "Army, fish, fowl." (See Noun)

Comparison

This term describes how adjectives are used to modify nouns. There are three degrees for all adjectives:

> *Positive:* good, quick, hungry
>
> *Comparative:* better, quicker, more hungry
>
> *Superlative:* best, quickest, most/very hungry

Complex Sentence

A sentence composed of an independent clause combined with one or more dependent clauses. (See Clause)

Compound Sentence

A sentence composed of more than one independent clauses. (See Clause)

Concrete Noun

A noun that refers to a tangible object, such as "tree" or "rock." (See Noun)

Conjugation

This term refers to orderly presentation of all the forms a verb can take in a given tense. This can happen at six points according to whether the subject of a verb is first, second, or third person (see Person) and whether the subject is singular or plural.

Example:　　I *am*　　　　we *are*

　　　　　　you *are*　　　you *are*

　　　　　　he/she/it *is*　they *are*

Conjunction

A word that connects things together in a sentence, either words or phrases or clauses. There are two major types of conjunctions, coordinating and subordinating.

A coordinating conjunction joins together items of similar or equal grammatical value. These are words such as *and, but, nor, or*.

Example: The master *and* the disciples.

Example: I went to the library *but* I did not check out a book.

A subordinating conjunction joins a subordinate or dependent clause (see clause) to an independent clause. These are words such as *when, if, although, because, since,* etc.

Example: I go to the library *if* I want to research a topic.

Example: *When* Jesus entered Capernaum, he healed the sick.

Dative

Here a noun is used as the indirect object in a sentence. (See Indirect Object) A noun in the dative case may have the word "to" or "for" preceding it. (See Case)

Example: The performer sang *them* a song. (The performer sang a song *for them*.)

Example: I gave the *child* a piece of cake. (I gave a piece of cake *to the child*.)

Declension

An orderly presentation of the forms a noun or pronoun can take in the various cases; vocative, nominative, genitive, dative, and accusative. (See Case) In English these variations are more common with pronouns than with nouns, but in Greek all nouns and pronouns as well as adjectives, participles, and articles will show distinctive forms for all the cases. Note the following four declensions listed side by side.

	Singular	Plural
Nominative	I / he / son / city	we / they / sons / cities
Genitive	my / his / son's / city's	our / their / sons' / cities'
Dative	me / him / son / city	us / them / sons / cities
Accusative	me / him / son / city	us / them / sons / cities

Demonstrative Pronouns and Demonstrative Adjectives

These are words that point to or identify particular nouns in a sentence. They are further classified as near demonstratives (this/these) or remote demonstratives (that/those).

> Demonstrative pronoun examples: *These* are the words of eternal life. *That* is the man.
>
> Demonstrative adjective examples: Give *this* bread to the hungry! I saw *those* Pharisees in the temple.

Dependent Clause

A clause which is an incomplete thought and must depend upon another clause to make a complete sentence. (See Clause)

Direct Discourse

When someone's exact words are presented, these words are said to be in direct discourse. In English direct discourse is identified by the presence of quotation marks. Contrast with indirect discourse, where the thoughts but not necessarily the exact words are presented.

> Example: Jesus said, "I am the way, the truth, and the life."
>
> Example: Jesus said that he is the way, the truth, and the life.

Direct Object

The noun or pronoun of a sentence that is directly affected by the verb.

> Example: The rabbi taught *the crowds*.
>
> Example: Jesus healed *the sick*.

Finite Verb

The term "finite" comes from the Latin word *finis* which means "boundary" or "limit." A finite verb is a verb which has a subject (is limited to or bound by a subject). Contrast this to an infinitive, which expresses a verbal idea that is not limited by ideas of time or subject.

> Example: "The people love to worship at the temple." Here the verbal idea "love" is limited to the subject and is a finite verb. In contrast, "to worship" is a verbal idea having no subject or reference to time and is therefore called an "infinitive."

Future

In English the future tense describes a future activity. (See Tenses)

Gender

In Greek, nouns and pronouns (with the associated adjectives and participles) are defined as masculine, feminine, or neuter.

> Examples: he / her / it; stallion / mare

In English gender describes the noun's sexual identity and therefore applies only to a limited number of nouns and pronouns. This is not the case in Greek, where all nouns and pronouns are given one of the three genders and this often without any reference to sexual identity.

Genitive

In Greek a genitive noun will express ownership or will in some way limit or further define the noun to which it is joined. It is often identified as a noun with an apostrophe or as a noun preceded by the word "of." (See Case)

> Example: The professor gave the *student's* book to a classmate.

> Example: One can find *men's* shoes in a department store.

> Example: I gave the child a piece *of cake*.

Gerund

A verb ending in "-ing" which is used as a noun.

> Example: The disciples loved *proclaiming* the words of Jesus.

Indefinite Pronoun

A pronoun that is non-specific or indefinite such as "some, any, few, other, several," etc.

> Example: *Some* will travel to Jerusalem.

Independent Clause

A clause which comprises a complete thought. (See Clause)

Indirect Discourse

When someone's words or ideas are presented without using the exact words, this is known as indirect discourse. Contrast with direct discourse, where a person is quoted exactly.

> Example: Jesus said, "I am the way, the truth, and the life."

> Example: Jesus said that he was the way, the truth, and the life.

Indirect Object

The noun in a sentence which is affected by the verbal activity indirectly.

> Example: The parent gave the child food. Here "food" is the direct object, the item actually given. "Child" is the indirect object since the child is still affected by the act of giving, but not in a direct way as with "food."

Infinitive

A verb that is not limited by a subject or reference to time. English infinitives commonly have the word "to" preceding them such as "to sing." See Finite Verb.

Inflection

A general term which denotes how words will take different forms depending upon how they are used in a sentence. These changes are made to identify number (singular and plural), gender, case, person, tense, mood, etc.

> Examples: he, his, him; walk, walked; go, went; fast, faster; mouse, mice; sing, sang, sung.

Intensive pronoun

A pronoun that emphasizes the antecedent. In English such pronouns are identified by the addition of the suffix "-self" or "-selves."

> Example: Jesus *himself* healed the crowds.

Interrogative Pronoun

A pronoun which introduces a question such as "who, where, which," etc.

> Examples: Where is the book? Who came to dinner? Why did you say that?

Intransitive Verb

This term applies to verbs which do not take direct objects. Instead, the verbal activity is confined to the subject.

> Examples: The man walked to town. The child grew. The wall fell.

By contrast, a *transitive verb* is one that takes a direct object. That is, the verbal activity is aimed at another noun in the sentence.

Examples: The man walked his dog. The child grew a flower.

Some verbs in English and Greek can be used both transitively and intransitively. Note the following:

Transitive: I sat the chair in the corner.

Intransitive: I sat in the corner.

Means

The means (thing) by which something is done.

Example: John baptized the people *with water*.

Modifier

A word with further qualifies, defines, or limits a noun a verb. Adjectives and adverbs are modifiers.

Mood

This term denotes how a verb is used in a sentence. A verb may be used to make a statement of fact, to express a wish, or to give a command. A verb may be used as a noun or as an adjective. A verb may also be used to express a hypothetical situation. All these different uses (moods) have distinctive labels in Greek.

- *Indicative mood*: statements of fact and questions.

    Example: Jesus *went* up to Jerusalem.

- *Subjunctive mood*: hypothetical statements.

    Example: If the disciple *goes* up to Jerusalem, he will teach in the temple courts.

- *Imperative mood*: commands or urgent requests.

    Example: *Go* up to Jerusalem

- *Infinitive mood*: a verb used as a noun.

    Example: The disciple loves *to go* up to Jerusalem.

- *Participial mood*: a verb used as an adjective.

    Example: The disciple *going* up to Jerusalem is the one who teaches in the temple courts.

Nominative

The case of the subject in a sentence. (See Case)

Noun

A person, place, or thing. Nouns are further classified in a variety of ways.

> A *proper noun* is the name of a person, place or thing. "John, Jerusalem."
>
> An *abstract noun* refers to a concept. "Love, joy, peace."
>
> A *collective noun* refers to group. "Army, fish, fowl."

Noun Clause

A noun clause is a combination of subject and predicate which functions as a subject or a direct object. That is, it takes the place of the subject or direct object. These will typically follow verbs of saying, thinking, believing, seeing, hearing, etc. (See Clause) Note the following examples:

> I see the teacher. (Here teacher is the direct object.)
>
> I see that the teacher is walking to class. (Here an entire clause functions as a direct object and is therefore called a noun clause.)

Number

The term which refers to whether a noun or pronoun is "singular" or "plural." "Dog, dogs."

Participle

One of the moods in Greek, where the verb functions like an adjective by modifying the noun to which it is joined.

> Example: The disciple *teaching* in the temple has studied the Torah.

Past Tense

A verb in English that refers to simple or repeated activities in past time. (See Tenses)

Passive Voice

When the subject of a sentence is being acted upon by someone or something else. (See Voice)

Perfect

A tense which describes a completed activity in the present. (See Tenses)

Person

A term which identifies either the speaker (first person), the one addressed (second person), or the one referenced (third person). These terms apply to verbs and pronouns.

- *Verbs:*

    I am walking (first person verb/the speaker is walking);

You are walking (second person verb/the one addressed is walking);

She is walking (third person verb/someone referenced is walking).

- *Pronouns:*

    I, me, we, us (first person/refers to the speaker)

    You (second person/the one addressed)

    He, him, she, her, it, they, them (third person/people or things referenced)

Personal Pronoun

A pronoun which refers to person or to people. (See Pronoun)

Pluperfect

A tense which refers to a completed activity in past time. (See Tenses)

Plural

A term which identifies that a noun or subject of a sentence is more than one. (See Number and Conjugation)

Positive

This term describes how adjectives are used to modify nouns. There are three degrees for all adjectives:

Positive: good, quick, hungry

Comparative: better, quicker, more hungry

Superlative: best, quickest, most/very hungry

Possessive Pronouns

These are pronouns with express an antecedent's ownership, words such are mine, yours, ours, his, hers, theirs.

Example: The books are *his*.

Predicate

All the things that are said about a subject in a clause or sentence. The predicate can be the verb alone such as "A man is walking." But the predicate also includes all the other information attached to a verb, such as "A man was walking into the temple very quickly the other day."

Predicate Adjective

An adjective that is joined to a noun by a verb such as "be" or "become." (See Adjective)

Predicate Noun

A noun which is part of the predicate and further describes the subject. Predicate nouns are commonly joined to the subject with the verbs "be" or "become."

Example: The Word was *God*.

Because predicate noun refers to the subject and further identifies it, the predicate noun also takes the nominative case. Hence the term *predicate nominative*.

Preposition

The word "preposition" literally means "placed before." It is a word that is joined to another word or words to make a phrase (prepositional phrase), and the phrase is then used to modify either a noun/pronoun or to modify a verb. There are a great variety of prepositions in English such as "under, with, by, over, at, beside, on, behind" and the like. Note the following examples:

The man *with the child* is singing.

The man is singing *with the child*.

In both these examples the prepositional phrase is "with the child." The phrase is comprised of a preposition, "with," and an object, "child." In the first example this phrase modifies the noun, further describing the man, and in the second example the phrase modifies the verb, further describing how the man was singing.

Prepositional Phrase

A preposition that is joined to another word or words to make a phrase, and the phrase is then used to modify either a noun/pronoun or to modify a verb. (See Preposition)

Present

A verb in English that refers to ongoing, customary, or repeated activity in the present. (See Tenses)

Primary Tense/Sequence

This term applies to indicative verbs expressing present or future time. Primary tenses in the indicative are the present, perfect, and future tenses. If the independent clause has a verb in a primary tense, any attached dependent clauses are said to be in primary sequence. See also Secondary Tense/Sequence.

Principle Parts

This term denotes the potential forms a verb might take throughout its conjugation in all tenses and moods. In English there are four principle parts: present, present participle, past, and past participle.

Example: walk, walking, walked, walked

Example: go, going, went, gone

Example: swim, swimming, swam, swum

There are potentially six principle parts for every Greek verb in the New Testament. These are: present active indicative, future active indicative, aorist active indicative, perfect active indicative, perfect middle/passive indicative, and aorist passive indicative.

Pronoun

A word that is used in place of a noun often to reduce repetition of the noun. Note the following:

> Example One: John went to John's house and John's wife met John at the door when she heard John approaching.

> Example Two: John went to his house and his wife met him at the door when she heard him coming.

Pronouns have a number of functions in a sentence. See the appropriate listing for each.

> *Demonstrative pronouns:* This, that, these
>
> *Indefinite pronouns:* a, any, some
>
> *Intensive pronouns:* myself, yourself, herself, ourselves
>
> *Interrogative pronouns:* Who? What? Whose?
>
> *Personal pronouns:* I, you, he, she, it, we, they
>
> *Possessive pronouns:* my, your, his, hers, its, our
>
> *Reflexive pronouns:* myself, yourself, herself, themselves
>
> *Relative pronouns:* who, which, that, whom, whose

Proper Noun

The name of a person, place, or thing. (See noun)

Reflexive Pronoun

A pronoun which "bends back" the activity of the verb to the subject. They are identified by the suffix "-self/-selves." (See Pronoun)

>Example: They taught *themselves* Greek.

>Example: He dressed *himself* for dinner.

Relative Clause

A combination of subject and predicate introduced by a relative pronoun. (See Relative Pronoun)

Relative Pronoun

A pronoun which introduces a clause and "relates" or connects it to an antecedent. The relative pronouns are who, which, that, whom, whose, etc.

>Example: "The person *who* teaches in the school is my cousin." The relative pronoun is "who." The relative clause is "...who teaches in the school." The antecedent is "person."

Secondary Tense/Sequence

This term applies to indicative verbs expressing past time, indicated by an augment on the verb. Secondary tenses in the indicative are the imperfect, pluperfect, and aorist tenses. If the dependent clause has a verb in a secondary tense, any attached dependent clauses are said to be in secondary sequence. See also Primary Tense/Sequence.

Singular

A term which identifies that a noun or subject of a sentence only one. (See Number and Conjugation)

Strong Verb

A verb whose stem will change with various tenses. By contrast, the stem of a weak verb will not change.

    Example: I walk, I walked, I have walked. (Weak verb)

    Example: I go, I went, I have gone (Strong verb)

Subordinate Clause

A clause which is an incomplete thought and must depend upon another clause to make a complete sentence. (See Clause)

Substantive

An adjective used as a noun. In Greek, definite articles, participles and prepositional phrases are used as substantives as well. (See Adjective)

Superlative

This term describes how adjectives are used to modify nouns. There are three degrees for all adjectives:

    Positive: good, quick, hungry

    Comparative: better, quicker, more hungry

    Superlative: best, quickest, most/very hungry

Tenses

In English the tense denotes the time of the verbal activity. Note the following:

    Present: I go, I am going

    Past: I went, I was going

    Future: I will go

Perfect: I have gone

Pluperfect: I had gone

Future Perfect: I will have gone

In Greek it is important to recognize that tense describes not primarily the time of the verbal activity but the type or aspect of the verbal activity. The major tenses in Greek are:

- *Present:* Continuous, habitual, repeated activity. The augment of the Imperfect casts this into the past. The Future casts this forward.
- *Aorist:* Momentary, punctiliar activity; or activity simply conceived
- *Perfect:* Completed activity with abiding results. The Pluperfect casts this activity into the past.

Transitive Verb

This term applies to verbs which take direct objects. That is, the verbal activity is aimed at another noun in the sentence.

Examples: The man walked his dog. The child grew a flower.

By contrast, an *intransitive verb* is one that does not take a direct object. Instead, the verbal activity is confined to the subject.

Examples: The man walked. The child grew. The wall fell.

Some verbs in English and Greek can be used both transitively and intransitively. Note the following:

Transitive: I sat the chair in the corner.

Intransitive: I sat in the corner.

Vocative

A noun is in the vocative case when it identifies the person or thing addressed. (See Case)

Example: *Professor*, can you explain this concept to me?

Example: *Lord*, please have mercy upon me!

Voice

This term describes whether the subject is acting upon something (active voice) or being acted upon (passive voice).

Example: The boy throws a ball. (Active voice)

Example: The boy is being thrown into the pool. (Passive voice)

Additionally, Greek has a middle voice. Here the subject does the verbal activity to itself or for itself. This middle voice in English is expressed by means of a reflexive pronoun.

Example: The boy throws himself into the pool. (Middle voice)

Weak Verb

A verb whose stem does not change with any given tense. By contrast, the stem of a strong verb will change with various tenses.

Example: I walk, I walked, I have walked. (Weak verb)

Example: I go, I went, I have gone (Strong verb)

2

Noun Cases

Greek has five noun cases, which define how nouns, pronouns, adjectives, and participles relate to each other in a sentence. The ancient Greeks pictured the nominative case, the case of the subject of a sentence, as standing upright and the others as falling or declining away. Hence the terms "declension" and "oblique" cases.

A. Vocative

The vocative is the case of direct address, as in "*O God*, hear my prayer." The vocative is often set apart in Greek by the presence of ὦ

> ὦ ἄνθρωπε, μενοῦνγε σὺ τίς εἶ ὁ ἀνταποκρινόμενος τῷ θεῷ;
> Rom 9:20
> "*O man*, who indeed are you, you who answer back to God?"

B. Nominative

The nominative case is the "naming" case. It identifies the subject of a sentence.

Noun Cases

1. Subject of a sentence

κἀγὼ δέ σοι λέγω ὅτι σὺ εἶ Πέτρος. Matt 16:18
"And I say to you that *you* are Peter."

2. Predicate Nominative

With verbs such as εἰμί, γίνομαι, etc., where the subject and "object" are the same, the "object" goes in the nominative case.

ἐν ἀρχῇ ἦν ὁ λόγος, καὶ ὁ λόγος ἦν πρὸς τὸν θεόν, καὶ θεὸς ἦν ὁ λόγος. John 1:1
"In the beginning was the word and the word was with God and the word was *God*."

C. Genitive

The genitive is the case of *separation* and of *description*. Of all the Greek cases, it shows the most variety of uses.

1. Possessive

The idea of ownership or possession can be expressed by the genitive case and is often best translated by an apostrophe with "s".

οἱ τοῦ Χριστοῦ 1 Cor 15:23
"*Christ's* people."

2. Source

That from which a noun or pronoun finds its origin or source may be placed in the genitive case. The genitive is often best translated as "from".

δικαιοσύνη γὰρ θεοῦ ἐν αὐτῷ ἀποκαλύπτεται Rom 1:17
"For righteousness *from* God is revealed in it."

3. Material

That of which a noun or pronoun is made may be expressed by the genitive case. The genitive is often best translated as "of" or "consisting of".

> οὐ γὰρ διὰ νόμου ἡ ἐπαγγελία τῷ Ἀβραὰμ ἢ τῷ σπέρματι αὐτοῦ . . . ἀλλὰ διὰ δικαιοσύνης πίστεως. Rom 4:13
> "For the promise did not belong to Abraham or his descendants through law . . . but through righteousness *of (consisting of) faith*."

4. Time "Within Which"

The time within which an action takes place is expressed by the genitive case without a preposition. The genitive is best translated as "within" or "during".

> οὗτος ἦλθεν πρὸς αὐτὸν νυκτὸς John 3:2
> "He came to him *during the night*."

5. Price

The price at which something sells may be expressed by the genitive case without a preposition. The genitive is best translated as "for".

> οὐχὶ δύο στρουθία ἀσσαρίου πωλεῖται; Matt 10:29
> "Two sparrows are sold *for a penny* aren't they?"

6. Definition

The genitive essentially modifies the noun or pronoun it accompanies and is best translated as an adjective.

> καὶ ἐπῄνεσεν ὁ κύριος τὸν οἰκονόμον τῆς ἀδικίας ὅτι φρονίμως ἐποίησεν Luke 16:8
> "And the master praised the *unjust* steward because he acted shrewdly."

7. Comparison

The second item of two things being compared may be placed in the genitive case. The genitive is best translated as "than".

ὁ δὲ ὀπίσω μου ἐρχόμενος ἰσχυρότερός μού ἐστιν Matt 3:11
"He who comes after me is mightier *than I*."

8. Partitive

The genitive may express the whole, from which a part is separated. The genitive is best translated as "from" or "of".

ἦσαν δέ τινες τῶν γραμματέων ἐκεῖ καθήμενοι Mark 2:6
"Now some *of the scribes* were sitting there."

9. Subjective / Objective

The difference between the subjective and objective genitives is best illustrated by the phrase "love of God". When the apostle states, "The love of God compels us," is he saying that God's love for them is compelling or that their love for God is compelling? The former is a subjective genitive (God is the subject of the love). The latter is an objective genitive (God is the object of the love). A clear example of the objective genitive would be Romans 3:25. Note how "justice" is the direct object of the verbal idea implicit in "proof."

ὃν προέθετο ὁ θεὸς ἱλαστήριον διὰ τῆς πίστεως ἐν τῷ αὐτοῦ αἵματι εἰς ἔνδειξιν τῆς δικαιοσύνης αὐτοῦ διὰ τὴν πάρεσιν τῶν προγεγονότων ἁμαρτημάτων. Rom 3:25

"Whom God put on public display as an atoning sacrifice through faith in his blood for a proof *of his justice* (in order to prove his justice) since he had passed over sins committed beforehand."

A clear example of the subjective genitive would be 1 Cor 1:18. Note how Christ is the subject of the verbal idea expressed in "love."

τίς ἡμᾶς χωρίσει ἀπὸ τῆς ἀγάπης τοῦ Χριστοῦ; 1 Cor 1:18
"Who will separate us from the love *of Christ* (from Christ loving us)?"

10. Genitive Absolute

A genitive noun or pronoun may be accompanied by a participle, also in the genitive case, to express a dependent (very often a temporal) clause.

> καὶ ἐκβληθέντος τοῦ δαιμονίου ἐλάλησεν ὁ κωφός. Matt 9:33
> "And *when the demon was cast out*, the one who was mute began to speak."

11. Apposition

Here the genitive is essentially the same thing as the noun it accompanies. It functions as a noun in apposition and is best translated as "that is".

> καὶ σημεῖον ἔλαβεν περιτομῆς σφραγῖδα τῆς δικαιοσύνης τῆς πίστεως τῆς ἐν τῇ ἀκροβυστίᾳ. Rom 4:11
> "And he received a sign, *that is, circumcision*, as a seal of his uncircumcised righteousness consisting of faith."

D. Dative

The dative is the case of *location*, *personal interest*, and *means* or *instrument*.

1. Means / Instrument

The impersonal means, tool, or instrument by which something is done may be placed in the dative case and is best translated as "with" or "by".

> τὸ δὲ ἄχυρον κατακαύσει πυρὶ ἀσβέστῳ. Matt 3:12
> "But the chaff he will burn *with an unquenchable fire*."

2. Indirect Object

Here the dative case generally indicates the person or thing which the verbal idea affects indirectly, such as "The teacher gave the book to the boy." Some grammars further subdivide this use of the dative into distinct categories such as the dative of advantage or disadvantage, and the dative of interest. All these usages can usually be translated by the English words "to" or "for".

ἀπὸ τότε ἤρξατο ὁ Ἰησοῦς δεικνύειν τοῖς μαθηταῖς αὐτοῦ ὅτι δεῖ αὐτὸν εἰς Ἱεροσόλυμα ἀπελθεῖν. Matt 16:21
"From that time Jesus began to show *his disciples* (to reveal *to his disciples*) that he must depart for Jerusalem."

ὁ γὰρ ἐσθίων καὶ πίνων κρίμα ἑαυτῷ ἐσθίει καὶ πίνει μὴ διακρίνων τὸ σῶμα. 1 Cor 11:29
"For the one who eats and drinks, since he does not discern the body, eats and drinks judgment *to himself* (against himself, a dative of disadvantage)."

εἴτε γὰρ ἐξέστημεν, θεῷ· εἴτε σωφρονοῦμεν, ὑμῖν. 2 Cor 5:13
"If we have lost our senses, *it is for God* (it is God's concern, a dative of interest); if we keep our heads about us, *it is for you* (it is for your benefit, a dative of advantage)."

3. Time When Something Occurs

This use of the dative is often best translated as "on" or "at".

τῇ τρίτῃ ἡμέρᾳ ἐγερθῆναι Matt 16:21
"To be raised *on the third day.*"

4. Possession

With εἰμί, γίνομαι or equivalent the dative may be used to denote the owner of the subject.

τί ὑμῖν δοκεῖ; ἐὰν γένηταί τινι ἀνθρώπῳ ἑκατὸν πρόβατα . . . Matt 18:12
"What do you think? *If a man had* one hundred sheep (if one hundred sheep belonged to a man), . . ."

5. Manner

The manner in which something happens may be indicated by the dative case and is often best translated as "with."

> εἰ ἐγὼ χάριτι μετέχω, τί βλασφημοῦμαι ὑπὲρ οὗ ἐγὼ εὐχαριστῶ; 1 Cor 10:30
> "If I partake (of it) *with thanksgiving*, why am I blasphemed concerning that for which I give thanks?"

6. Reference

The sphere in which something holds true or takes place is often denoted by the dative case and is often best translated as "in regard to" or simply "to".

> οὕτως καὶ ὑμεῖς λογίζεσθε ἑαυτοὺς [εἶναι] νεκροὺς μὲν τῇ ἁμαρτίᾳ ζῶντας δὲ τῷ θεῷ ἐν Χριστῷ Ἰησοῦ. Rom 6:11
> "So you also, consider yourselves to be dead *in regard to sin* but alive *to God* in Christ Jesus."

7. Agent with Passive Verbs

The person by whose authority or power an action takes place may be expressed by the dative if the main verb is in the passive voice. Otherwise, agency is expressed by ὑπό with the genitive case. This dative is often best translated as "by," or else the agent should be turned into the subject of an active sentence.

> ἰδοὺ οὐδὲν ἄξιον θανάτου ἐστὶν πεπραγμένον αὐτῷ· Luke 23:15
> "Look, nothing deserving death has been done *by him*."
> "Look, he has done nothing deserving death."

E. Accusative

The accusative case *receives movement* and is therefore the case of the direct object. The accusative can also express the *extent of time and space*.

Noun Cases

1. Cognate Accusative

An accusative that comes from the same root as the verb is a cognate accusative. This construction is used for emphasis and is often best translated by an appropriate adverb.

> ἰδόντες δὲ τὸν ἀστέρα ἐχάρησαν χαρὰν μεγάλην σφόδρα. Matt 2:10
>
> "And when they saw the star, they rejoiced *greatly*." Literally, "*They rejoiced a great joy.*"

2. Direct Object

The direct object of a sentence is placed in the accusative case.

> καὶ ἐξελθὼν εἶδεν πολὺν ὄχλον. Matt 14:14
>
> "And after he left, he saw *a large crowd.*"

3. Two Accusatives with One Verb

Verbs of asking, teaching, swearing, doing good, etc. may take two accusatives.

> καὶ ἤρξατο διδάσκειν αὐτοὺς πολλα. Mark 6:34
>
> "And he began to teach *them many things.*"

4. Adverbial Accusative

Neuter pronouns and adjectives in the accusative case may also serve as adverbs and are often best translated as such.

> καὶ ῥῖψαν αὐτὸν τὸ δαιμόνιον εἰς τὸ μέσον ἐξῆλθεν ἀπ' αὐτοῦ μηδὲν βλάψαν αὐτόν. Luke 4:35
>
> "And throwing him into their midst, the demon came out of him, *in no way* harming him."

5. Extent of Time or Space

The duration of an activity or the extent of space may be expressed by the accusative case and is best translated as "for".

> καὶ ἐκεῖ ἔμειναν οὐ πολλὰς ἡμέρας. John 2:12
> "And they did not remain there *for many days.*"

6. Subject of an Infinitive

The subject of an infinitive is always placed in the accusative case unless the subject of the infinitive is also the subject of the main sentence.

> ὁ οὖν ὄχλος ὁ ἑστὼς καὶ ἀκούσας ἔλεγεν βροντὴν γεγονέναι John 12:29
> "Therefore, the crowd, which was standing around and had heard, were *saying that it had thundered (that thunder had occurred).*"

7. Accusative of Respect

The sphere in which the verbal action takes place or holds true may be expressed by the accusative and is often best translated as "in regard/respect to".

> πᾶς δὲ ὁ ἀγωνιζόμενος πάντα ἐγκρατεύεται. 1 Cor 9:25
> "Now every contestant exercises self-control *in respect to all things.*"

3

Syntax of the Greek Article

The article in Greek serves generally to identify, emphasize, give substance to, or point to something be it a noun, pronoun, adjective, or participle. Accordingly, it is also used as a marker for syntax, identifying how modifiers are to be connected with their nouns.

A. Articles with Nouns

1. With Proper Names

Unlike English, the proper names of people or locations may take the article. The practice is inconsistent in the New Testament, and there is no agreement as to whether the presence or absence of the article appreciably changes the emphasis of a given name.

> εἶπεν δὲ Πέτρος· ἀργύριον καὶ χρυςίον οὐχ ὑπάρχει μοι.
> Acts 3:6
> "And Peter said, 'I have no silver or gold.'"

> ὁ Πέτρος λέγει τῷ Ἰησοῦ· ῥαββί, καλόν ἐστιν ἡμᾶς ὧδε εἶναι.
> Mark 9:5
> "Peter says to Jesus, 'Rabbi, it is good that we are here.'"

2. With Abstract Nouns

Unlike English, abstract nouns in Greek will normally take the article.

> ἡ γνῶσις φυσιοῖ, ἡ δὲ ἀγάπη οἰκοδομεῖ. 1 Cor 8:1
> "Knowledge brings conceit, love builds."

3. Demonstrative Article

The article can identify something already referenced in a given literary or situational context. It is often best translated with a demonstrative pronoun.

> ὅσοι ἐβαπτίσθημεν εἰς Χριστὸν Ἰησοῦν, εἰς τὸν θάνατον αὐτοῦ ἐβαπτίσθημεν; συνετάφημεν οὖν αὐτῷ διὰ τοῦ βαπτίσματος εἰς τὸν θάνατον. Rom 6:3-4
> "(Do you not know that) as many of us who were baptized into Christ Jesus where baptized into his death. Therefore, we were buried with him through *this* baptism into death."

4. Possessive Article

The article can be used in place of a possessive pronoun when the context clearly indicates such.

> οἱ ἄνδρες, ἀγαπᾶτε τὰς γυναῖκας, καθὼς καὶ ὁ Χριστὸς ἠγάπησεν τὴν ἐκκλησίαν. Eph 5:25
> "You husbands, love *your* wives just as Christ also loved *his* Church!"

B. Articles as Pronouns

The article may regularly take the place of a pronoun. This is especially common in narrative.

> ὁ δὲ οὐκ ἀπεκρίθη αὐτῇ λόγον. Matt 15:23
> "But *he* gave her no response."

> οἱ δὲ εἶπαν· τί ἔτι ἔχομεν μαρτυρίας χρείαν; Luke 22:71
> "And *they* said, 'Why do we need any more testimony?'"

C. Articles as Substantives

The article may take the place of a noun particularly when the noun is generic or may be easily supplied from the context.

> οἴδαμεν δὲ ὅτι ὅσα ὁ νόμος λέγει τοῖς ἐν τῷ νόμῳ λαλεῖ.
> Rom 3:19
> "But we know that whatever the law says, it speaks to *people* who are in that law."

D. Articles as Syntactical Markers

With modifiers, the presence or absence of the articular will indicate whether the modifier is to be translated with a noun/pronoun (similar to an adjective) or to be translated as part of the verb (similar to an adverb). A modifier which is joined directly to a noun/pronoun by the article is said to be in the attributive position. Conversely, a modifier without the article is generally translated with the verb and is said to be in the predicate position. Note the following examples for the prepositional phrase "in the house." In the first example the phrase modifies a noun while in the second the phrase is translated with the verb.

> "The man in the house is singing." *Attributive position*
> "The man is singing in the house." *Predicate position*

This is also the case with adjectives and participles.

> "The talented man is singing." *Attributive adjective*
> "The man is talented." *Predicate adjective*

> "The singing man (man who is singing) came into the house." *Attributive participle*
> "The man came into the house singing." *Predicate participle*

In Greek, the presence of the article before the modifier (adjective, prepositional phrase, participle) will indicate the attributive use of the modifier. Its absence will generally indicate the predicate use. Note the following examples.

1. Adjectives

In the following example, note which adjectives have articles! "Narrow" is an attributive adjective. "Wide" and "broad" are predicate adjectives.

> εἰσέλθατε διὰ τῆς στενῆς πύλης· ὅτι πλατεῖα ἡ πύλη καὶ εὐρύχωρος ἡ ὁδὸς ἡ ἀπάγουσα εἰς τὴν ἀπώλειαν. Matt 7:13
> "Enter through the narrow gate; because the gate is wide and the road leading to destruction is broad."

2. Prepositional phrases

In the following example, note the presence of the article before the prepositional phrase! This places the phrase in the attributive position with "Father." Literally, "Glorify your in-the-heavens father!"

> δοξάσωσιν τὸν πατέρα ὑμῶν τὸν ἐν τοῖς οὐρανοῖς. Matt 5:16
> "They will glorify your Father who is in heaven."

In the next example, the article does not precede the prepositional phrase, indicating that the phrase is in the predicate position and therefore further modifies the verb.

> χαίρετε δὲ ὅτι τὰ ὀνόματα ὑμῶν ἐγγέγραπται ἐν τοῖς οὐρανοῖς. Luke 10:20
> "But rejoice because your names are written in heaven!"

3. Participles

In this first example, the participle, "dwell," is in the attributive position, indicating that it modifies the noun in the same number, gender, and case. Literally, "The dwelling-in-me sin is producing it."

> οὐκέτι ἐγὼ κατεργάζομαι αὐτὸ ἀλλὰ ἡ οἰκοῦσα ἐν ἐμοὶ ἁμαρτία. Rom 7:20
> "I myself am not still producing it but the sin which dwells in me."

In the next example, the participle, "see," is in the predicate position and therefore should not be translated with the subject—"The men who saw the star rejoiced"—but with the verb as a dependent clause.

> ἰδόντες δὲ τὸν ἀστέρα ἐχάρησαν χαρὰν μεγάλην σφόδρα.
> Matt 2:10
> "And they were overjoyed when they saw the star."

For more information, see below under Participles!

4

Tenses of the Verb

A. Tense Aspect

Greek tenses denote the type of action, further delineated as aspect and *Aktionsart*, and not primarily the time of action. This is true particularly for the subjunctive, optative, imperative, infinitive, and participle moods. In these moods the tenses have temporal significance only in relation to the main verb or when they are used in indirect statements. In all other respects the tenses express primarily a particular type of verbal action. Even in the indicative, where the tenses have temporal significance, the type of verbal activity is still primary.

1. The Present

The present tense denotes continuous, repeated, or on-going action.

Examples: I teach. (repeated activity)

I breath. (continuous activity)

I am writing. (on-going activity)

2. The Aorist

The aorist tense denotes punctiliar action or action which happens over a period of time but is simply conceived without emphasizing its continuance or results.

Examples: I taught piano for ten years. (repeated action simply conceived)

I taught a piano lesson yesterday. (punctiliar action)

3. The Perfect

The perfect tense denotes completed action with abiding results.

Examples: I have died. (completed action)

I am dead. (abiding results)

B. Tenses in the Indicative

In the indicative the augment signals past time, not the tense. For example, the aorist indicative, imperfect indicative, and pluperfect indicative all have temporal augments and therefore are all past tenses. They differ from each other according to the type of action they express. The imperfect denotes continuous past activity, the aorist simple or one time past activity, and the pluperfect completed past activity.

1. Present: Continuous Action in the Present

a. Progressive Present

The present tense denotes an action which is taking place at the moment of speaking.

δότε ἡμῖν ἐκ τοῦ ἐλαίου ὑμῶν, ὅτι αἱ λαμπάδες ἡμῶν σβέννυνται. Matt 25:8

"Give us some of your oil because our lamps *are going out*."

b. Present of General Truth (Gnomic Present)

The present tense denotes something which is generally true but which may or may not be happening at the moment. It is often called the gnomic present because it is one of the tenses for proverbial (gnomic) sayings.

> οὕτως πᾶν δένδρον ἀγαθὸν καρποὺς καλοὺς ποιεῖ. Matt 7:17
> "In the same way every good true *produces* good fruit."

c. Present of Customary or Repeated Action

The present tense denotes something that happens repeatedly.

> καθ' ἡμέραν ἀποθνῄσκω. 1 Cor 15:31
> "I *die* each day."

d. Conative Present

The present tense denotes something which is attempted but not attained.

> πολλὰ ἔργα καλὰ ἔδειξα ὑμῖν ἐκ τοῦ πατρός· διὰ ποῖον αὐτῶν ἔργον ἐμὲ λιθάζετε; John 10:32
> "Many good deeds I showed you from the father; for which of these *are you trying to stone* me?"

e. Historic Present

The present tense is used for a past action to make the action more vivid. This use of the present is especially prevalent in the Gospels.

> καὶ ἔρχονται πάλιν εἰς Ἱεροσόλυμα. Mark 11:27
> "And *they come (came)* again into Jerusalem."

Tenses of the Verb

2. Imperfect: Continuous Action in the Past

a. Progressive Action: lengthy occurrence in past time.

Καὶ καθίσας κατέναντι τοῦ γαζοφυλακίου ἐθεώρει πῶς ὁ ὄχλος βάλλει χαλκὸν εἰς τὸ γαζοφυλάκιον. Mark 12:41
"And sitting opposite the moneybox, *he was watching* how the crowd was dropping money into the box."

b. Repeated Action: a regularly occurring or repeated action in the past time.

ὃν ἐτίθουν καθ' ἡμέραν πρὸς τὴν θύραν τοῦ ἱεροῦ. Acts 3:2
"Whom *they were placing* each day beside the temple door."

c. Conative Imperfect: something attempted but not attained in past time.

ὁ δὲ Ἰωάννης διεκώλυεν αὐτόν. Matt 3:14
"But John *was trying to prevent* him."

3. Aorist: Simple Action in the Past

a. Historic Aorist

1. Momentary Action: a one-time event.

   ἀκούων δὲ ὁ Ἀνανίας τοὺς λόγους τούτους πεσὼν ἐξέψυξεν. Acts 5:5
   "And while he was listening to these words, Ananias fell down and *died*."

2. Comprehensive: a continued state viewed simply as a single entity.

   ὁ δὲ θεὸς πλούσιος ὢν ἐν ἐλέει, διὰ τὴν πολλὴν ἀγάπην αὐτοῦ ἣν ἠγάπησεν ἡμᾶς . . . Eph 2:4
   "But God, because he is rich in mercy and on account of his great love, which *he showed* us. . ."

3. Collective: a series of acts viewed simply as one.

> ἐν τῇ ἀναστάσει οὖν τίνος τῶν ἑπτὰ ἔσται γυνή; πάντες γὰρ ἔσχον αὐτήν· Matt 22:28
> "Therefore at the resurrection whose wife will the woman be? For all *had* her (as a wife)."

b. Inceptive/Ingressive Aorist

The aorist may be used to stress the beginning of the verbal action and in such cases is best translated as "began to".

> ὅτι δι' ὑμᾶς ἐπτώχευσεν πλούσιος ὤν, ἵνα ὑμεῖς τῇ ἐκείνου πτωχείᾳ πλουτήσητε. 2 Cor 8:9
> "Although he was rich, for your sake *he became (began to be) poor* so that you *might become rich (begin to be rich)* by his poverty."

c. Gnomic Aorist

The aorist is sometimes used to express a proverbial (gnomic) saying and is best translated by a present tense.

> διότι πᾶσα σὰρξ ὡς χόρτος καὶ πᾶσα δόξα αὐτῆς ὡς ἄνθος χόρτου· ἐξηράνθη ὁ χόρτος καὶ τὸ ἄνθος ἐξέπεσεν. 1 Pet 1:24
> "Because all flesh is like grass and all its glory like a flower of the field; the grass *withers* and the flower *falls*."

d. Epistolary Aorist

An author of a letter might use the aorist to describe something which at the time of writing occurs in the present.

> ὃν ἔπεμψα πρὸς ὑμᾶς εἰς αὐτὸ τοῦτο. Eph 6:22
> "Whom *I am sending (I sent)* to you for this purpose."

4. Future

a. Simple Action

As with the present, the future tense may be used to express actions in a simple way, that is, without any reference to their duration.

> σαλπίσει γὰρ καὶ οἱ νεκροὶ ἐγερθήσονται. 1 Cor 15:52
> "For *the trumpet will sound*, and the dead *will be raised*."

b. Progressive, Continuing Action

As with the present, the future also expresses activities which continue over a period of time.

> Χριστὸς καταγγέλλεται, καὶ ἐν τούτῳ χαίρω. ἀλλὰ καὶ χαρήσομαι. Phil 1:18
> "Christ is proclaimed, and in this I rejoice. But also I *will continue rejoicing*."

5. Perfect

At heart the perfect expresses actions which have just been completed so that the results still abide in the present. The translator must often choose whether it is better to emphasize the completeness of the action, as in "it has been written", or the abiding result, as in "it is written".

a. Completed Action

> τὸν καλὸν ἀγῶνα ἠγώνισμαι, τὸν δρόμον τετέλεκα, τὴν πίστιν τετήρηκα. 2 Tim 4:7
> "*I have fought* the good fight, *I have finished* the race, *I have kept* the faith."

b. Abiding Result

ὅτε οὖν ἔλαβεν τὸ ὄξος ὁ Ἰησοῦς εἶπεν· τετέλεσται. John 19:30
"So when Jesus took the sour wine, he said, 'It is complete.'"

6. Pluperfect

The pluperfect carries the meaning of the perfect into past time; that is, completed action in the past with an abiding result in the past.

a. Completed Action

καὶ ὧδε εἰς τοῦτο ἐληλύθει; Acts 9:21
"And *had he not come* here for this purpose?"

b. Abiding Result

καὶ ἐπιτιμῶν οὐκ εἴα αὐτὰ λαλεῖν, ὅτι ᾔδεισαν τὸν χριστὸν αὐτὸν εἶναι. Luke 4:41
"And he was rebuking them and was not allowing them to speak because *they knew* that he was the Messiah."

C. Tenses in Indirect Statements

The tenses of indirect statements have temporal significance and should be translated as such. Note how the infinitive is translated in the following examples.

ὁ ἄνθρωπος λέγει τὸν ἀπόστολον βαπτίζειν τοὺς πιστεύοντες
"The man says that the apostle *is baptizing* the believers."

ὁ ἄνθρωπος λέγει τὸν ἀπόστολον βαπτίσειν τοὺς πιστεύοντες
"The man says that the apostle *will baptize* the believers."

ὁ ἄνθρωπος λέγει τὸν ἀπόστολον βαπτίσαι τοὺς πιστεύοντες
"The man says that the apostle *baptized* the believers."

Tenses of the Verb

The temporal significance of the verb in the indirect statement depends upon the tense of the main verb. That is, if the main verb is a secondary tense, the verb of the indirect statement will be translated accordingly. Note the following examples.

ὁ ἄνθρωπος λέγει τὸν ἀπόστολον βαπτίζειν τοὺς πιστεύοντες
"The man *says* that the apostle *is baptizing* the believers."

ὁ ἄνθρωπος εἶπεν τὸν ἀπόστολον βαπτίζειν τοὺς πιστεύοντες
"The man *said* that the apostle *was baptizing* the believers."

ὁ ἄνθρωπος λέγει τὸν ἀπόστολον βαπτίσειν τοὺς πιστεύοντες
"The man *says* that the apostle *will baptize* the believers."

ὁ ἄνθρωπος εἶπεν τὸν ἀπόστολον βαπτίσειν τοὺς πιστεύοντες
"The man *said* that the apostle *would baptize* the believers."

5

Voices of the Verb

A. Active Voice

In the active voice the subject performs the action. Active verbs can be either transitive or intransitive. Transitive verbs take a direct object because the action of the verb is performed upon or directed toward something.

>Example: I stood the chair in the corner.

Intransitive verbs do not take a direct object because the verbal activity is confined to the subject.

>Example: I stood in the corner.

B. Middle Voice

In the middle voice the subject acts upon itself, for itself, or has something done in its own interest.

1. Direct Reflexive

The subject here acts upon itself.

>καὶ ἀπελθὼν ἀπήγξατο. Matt 27:5
>"(Judas) left and *hung himself.*"

2. Indirect Reflexive

The subject acts not upon but for itself or in its own interest.

> ἐξελέξατο ἡμᾶς ἐν αὐτῷ πρὸ καταβολῆς κόσμου εἶναι ἡμᾶς ἁγίους καὶ ἀμώμους κατενώπιον αὐτοῦ. Eph 1:4
> "He chose us *(for his own purposes)* in him before the foundation of the world that we be holy and blameless before him."

3. Causative

The subject has something done (by another) for or to himself or herself.

> ὄφελον καὶ ἀποκόψονται οἱ ἀναστατοῦντες ὑμᾶς. Gal 5:12
> "I wish that those who trouble you would *have themselves castrated!*"

C. Passive Voice

In the passive voice the subject is inactive (passive), being acted upon by an impersonal means or by a personal agent. Impersonal means is often expressed by ἐν with the dative or by the simple dative alone whereas personal agency is most often expressed by ὑπό followed by the genitive. Note the following examples:

> παρακαλούμεθα αὐτοὶ ὑπὸ τοῦ θεοῦ. 2 Cor 1:4
> "We ourselves are comforted by God."

> λογιζόμεθα γὰρ δικαιοῦσθαι πίστει ἄνθρωπον χωρὶς ἔργων νόμου. Rom 3:28
> "For we consider a man to be justified by faith apart from works of Law."

D. Middle Only Verbs (Deponent)

Many verbs have only middle/passive endings. Note also that some verbs exhibit exclusively middle endings in certain principle parts.

ἔρχομαι, ἐλεύσομαι, ἦλθον, ἐλήλυθα

ἐσθίω, φάγομαι, ἔφαγον

Such verbs or principle parts have traditionally been labeled as deponent since it was thought that these verbs had "laid aside" their active endings while retaining their original (active) meanings. More recent research has brought this concept into question, and so it may be better to label these as "middle only" verbs.

6

Indicative Mood

The verbs in the indicative mood express reality. As such, the indicative mood is for statements of fact and for questions.

A. Independent Clauses

1. Simple Declarations.

This is the most common use for the indicative mood.

> καὶ ἐξῆλθεν πάλιν παρὰ τὴν θάλασσαν· καὶ πᾶς ὁ ὄχλος ἤρχετο πρὸς αὐτόν, καὶ ἐδίδασκεν αὐτούς. Mark 2:13
> "And he went out again alongside the lake; and the entire crowd was coming to him, and he was teaching them."

2. Questions

The indicative mood is regularly used to ask questions when an answer is expected.

> σὺ εἶ ὁ χριστὸς ὁ υἱὸς τοῦ εὐλογητοῦ; Mark 14:61
> "Are you the Messiah, the son of the Blessed One?"

If the person posing the question expects a positive reply, the question will be cast with οὐ. Alternatively, if a negative reply is expected, the question will be cast with μή.

οὐκ οἴδατε ὅτι ναὸς θεοῦ ἐστε καὶ τὸ πνεῦμα τοῦ θεοῦ οἰκεῖ ἐν ὑμῖν; 1Cor 3:16
"Do you not know that you are a temple of God and that the Spirit of God dwells in you?" (You do know, don't you, that...)

μὴ δύναται ἡ πίστις σῶσαι αὐτόν; Jas 2:14
"That faith cannot save him, can it?"

B. Conditional Statements

The indicative is used both for first class and second class conditional statements. (See below for an overview of conditional statements).

1. Simple Conditions (First Class Conditions)

εἰ δὲ ἐν πνεύματι θεοῦ ἐγὼ ἐκβάλλω τὰ δαιμόνια, ἄρα ἔφθασεν ἐφ᾽ ὑμᾶς ἡ βασιλεία τοῦ θεοῦ. Matt 12:28
"But if I myself cast out demons with the Spirit of God, truly the kingdom of God has come upon you."

2. Present and Past Contrary to Fact Conditions (Second Class Conditions)

εἰ ὁ θεὸς πατὴρ ὑμῶν ἦν ἠγαπᾶτε ἂν ἐμέ. John 8:42
If God were your father, you would love me.

καὶ εἰ μὴ ἐκολοβώθησαν αἱ ἡμέραι ἐκεῖναι, οὐκ ἂν ἐσώθη πᾶσα σάρξ. Matt 24:22
"And if those days had not been cut short, no flesh would have survived."

Indicative Mood

C. With ὅτι

ὅτι clauses introduce an indicative in two broad ways. The first is to introduce a causal clause. The second is to introduce a noun clause which can itself then serve as the subject or object of a sentence or stand in apposition to some other noun or pronoun in the sentence.

1. Causal Clauses

καὶ ἡμεῖς εἰς Χριστὸν Ἰησοῦν ἐπιστεύσαμεν, ἵνα δικαιωθῶμεν ἐκ πίστεως Χριστοῦ καὶ οὐκ ἐξ ἔργων νόμου, ὅτι ἐξ ἔργων νόμου οὐ δικαιωθήσεται πᾶσα σάρξ. Gal 2:16
"And we ourselves have placed our trust in Christ Jesus in order to be justified from faith and not from works of law because no flesh will be justified from works of law."

2. Noun Clauses

As an object clause ὅτι commonly follows verbs of saying, speaking, thinking, knowing, and the like.

κἀγὼ δέ σοι λέγω ὅτι σὺ εἶ Πέτρος. Matt 16:18
"And I say to you that you are Peter."

λέγει αὐτῷ ἡ Μάρθα· οἶδα ὅτι ἀναστήσεται ἐν τῇ ἀναστάσει ἐν τῇ ἐσχάτῃ ἡμέρᾳ. John 11:24
"Martha said to him, 'I know that he will rise in the resurrection on the last day.'"

Commonly ὅτι will be used similarly to introduce indirect and direct statements. With direct statements, ὅτι is best translated as a quotation mark. Note the following examples:

ἄλλοι ἔλεγον ὅτι οὗτός ἐστιν, ἄλλοι ἔλεγον· οὐχί, ἀλλὰ ὅμοιος αὐτῷ ἐστιν. ἐκεῖνος ἔλεγεν ὅτι ἐγώ εἰμι. John 9:9
"Some were saying, 'This is the guy.' Others were saying, 'No! He just resembles him.' The man was saying, 'I'm the guy.'"

σὺ λέγεις ὅτι βασιλεύς εἰμι. John 18:37
"You say that I am a king."

A ὅτι noun clause can stand in apposition to a noun or pronoun.

αὕτη δέ ἐστιν ἡ κρίσις ὅτι τὸ φῶς ἐλήλυθεν εἰς τὸν κόσμον καὶ ἠγάπησαν οἱ ἄνθρωποι μᾶλλον τὸ σκότος ἢ τὸ φῶς. John 3:19
"This is the judgment, that light has come into the world and men loved darkness more than the light."

7

Subjunctive Mood

At heart the subjunctive mood is the mood of hypothetical constructions and thus is the mood often encountered in dependent clauses. In the New Testament the subjunctive mood generally retains its Classical and Hellenistic functions but also takes on many uses of the simple and articular infinitive when used with ἵνα. Additionally, it is occasionally used for the future indicative.

A. Hortatory

Meaning: A first person command.
Identification: The subjunctive is the verb of an independent, non-interrogative clause and will be in the first person.

> *Example:* δι' ὑπομονῆς τρέχωμεν τὸν προκείμενον ἡμῖν ἀγῶνα. Heb 12:1
> "*Let us run* with endurance the race which is before us!"

B. Deliberative

Meaning: The subject asks what he/she/it should do or what is to be done. The question is asked about that which is possible, necessary, or desirable.
Identification: The subjunctive is the verb of an independent, interrogative clause.

Example: πῶς οὖν ἐπικαλέσωνται εἰς ὃν οὐκ ἐπίστευσαν; Rom 10:14

"How therefore *can they call* on one in whom they did not believe?"

C. Prohibitions

Meaning: The aorist subjunctive is used with μή as a negative command or prohibition. Note that the present imperative with μή is also used as a prohibition, the difference being that the aorist subjunctive is most frequently used to forbid an activity that has not yet begun. The present imperative, by contrast, forbids the continuance of an activity already begun.

Identification: The subjunctive, preceded by the negative particle, is the verb of an independent clause.

Example: μὴ οὖν μεριμνήσητε εἰς τὴν αὔριον. Matt 6:34

"Therefore, *do not worry* about tomorrow!"

D. ἵνα Plus Subjunctive

In Classical Greek and generally in Hellenistic Greek, ἵνα with the subjunctive expresses purpose, but in the New Testament this construction also expresses many of the same ideas as the simple and articular infinitive. These expanded uses are especially prevalent in John's gospel and letters.

1. Purpose

μὴ κρίνετε, ἵνα μὴ κριθῆτε. Matt 7:1

"Do not judge *in order that you not be judged.*"

2. Result

τίς ἥμαρτεν, οὗτος ἢ οἱ γονεῖς αὐτοῦ, ἵνα τυφλὸς γεννηθῇ; John 9:2

"Who sinned, this man or his parents, *with the result that* he was born blind?"

ἐὰν ὁμολογῶμεν τὰς ἁμαρτίας ἡμῶν, πιστός ἐστιν καὶ δίκαιος, ἵνα ἀφῇ ἡμῖν τὰς ἁμαρτίας καὶ καθαρίσῃ ἡμᾶς ἀπὸ πάσης ἀδικίας. 1 John 1:9

"If we confess our sins, he is faithful and just *with the result that he forgives* our sins and *cleanses* us from all unrighteousness."

καὶ οὐδεὶς ἐξ αὐτῶν ἀπώλετο εἰ μὴ ὁ υἱὸς τῆς ἀπωλείας, ἵνα ἡ γραφὴ πληρωθῇ. John 17:12

"And not one of them was lost except the son of destruction, *with the result that* scripture was fulfilled."

3. Subject or Object of a Sentence

ὧδε λοιπὸν ζητεῖται ἐν τοῖς οἰκονόμοις, ἵνα πιστός τις εὑρεθῇ. 1 Cor 4:2

"In this area, finally, what is sought among administrators is *that one be found faithful.*"

ἐμὸν βρῶμά ἐστιν ἵνα ποιήσω τὸ θέλημα τοῦ πέμψαντός με. John 4:34

"My food is *to do the will of him who sent me.*"

4. Apposition

αὕτη γάρ ἐστιν ἡ ἀγάπη τοῦ θεοῦ, ἵνα τὰς ἐντολὰς αὐτοῦ τηρῶμεν. 1 John 5:3

"For this is love for God, *that we keep his commandments.*"

5. Explanatory/Complementary

τίς σοι ἔδωκεν τὴν ἐξουσίαν ταύτην ἵνα ταῦτα ποιῇς; Mark 11:28

"Who gave you this authority *to do* these things?"

Ἀβραὰμ ὁ πατὴρ ὑμῶν ἠγαλλιάσατο ἵνα ἴδῃ τὴν ἡμέραν τὴν ἐμήν. John 8:56

"Abraham, your father, rejoiced *to see* my day."

E. Future More Vivid Constructions

Meaning: A condition or other statement about the future or a statement which concerns a hypothetical situation. The statement is vivid in the mind of the speaker.

Identification: ἐάν (or equivalent) + subjunctive in the protasis, future indicative in the apodosis.

> *Examples:* ἐάν τις φάγῃ ἐκ τούτου τοῦ ἄρτου ζήσει εἰς τὸν αἰῶνα. John 6:51
>
> "If someone eats from this bread, he will live forever."
>
> ὅταν δὲ ἔλθῃ ὁ υἱὸς τοῦ ἀνθρώπου ἐν τῇ δόξῃ αὐτοῦ καὶ πάντες οἱ ἄγγελοι μετ' αὐτοῦ, τότε καθίσει ἐπὶ θρόνου δόξης αὐτοῦ. Matt 25:31
>
> "When the son of man comes in his glory and all his angels with him, then he will sit upon his glorious throne."
>
> ὃς γὰρ ἂν θέλῃ τὴν ψυχὴν αὐτοῦ σῶσαι ἀπολέσει αὐτήν· ὃς δ' ἂν ἀπολέσῃ τὴν ψυχὴν αὐτοῦ ἕνεκεν ἐμοῦ οὗτος σώσει αὐτήν. Luke 9:24
>
> "For the one who desires to save his soul will lose it; but the one who loses his soul for my sake will save it."

F. Present General Constructions

Meaning: A condition or other statement that is generally true in present time.

Identification: ἐάν (or equivalent) + subjunctive in the protasis, present indicative in the apodosis.

> *Examples:* ἐὰν εἴπωμεν ὅτι ἁμαρτίαν οὐκ ἔχομεν, ἑαυτοὺς πλανῶμεν. 1 John 1:8
>
> "If (ever) we say that we have no sin, we deceive ourselves."

Subjunctive Mood

μακάριοί ἐστε ὅταν ὀνειδίσωσιν ὑμᾶς καὶ διώξωσιν καὶ εἴπωσιν πᾶν πονηρὸν καθ' ὑμῶν ἕνεκεν ἐμοῦ. Matt 5:11
"You are blessed when(ever) they reproach you and persecute you and speak all evil against you because of me."

ὃς ἂν ποιήσῃ τὸ θέλημα τοῦ θεοῦ, οὗτος ἀδελφός μου καὶ ἀδελφὴ καὶ μήτηρ ἐστίν. Mark 3:35
"The one who does the will of my father, this one is my brother and sister and mother."

G. Fear Clauses

Meaning: The subjunctive is employed in a clause which states a fear about the future. The verb of fearing will normally be in a primary (present, future, perfect) tense. Note that the fear clause is idiomatically introduced by μή, which should not translated as a negative.

Identification: φοβέομαι (or equivalent) μή + subjunctive

Example: φοβοῦμαι γὰρ μή πως ἐλθὼν οὐχ οἵους θέλω εὕρω ὑμᾶς. 2 Cor 12:20
"For I am afraid *that (lest)* after I come *I will find* that somehow you are not as I wish."

8

Optative Mood

One of the characteristic features of New Testament Greek is the retreat of the optative from regular use. Whereas in classical Greek the optative would regularly be found for verbs in dependent clauses in secondary sequence, this no longer holds true for the New Testament.

We find the optative only sixty-eight times in the New Testament with Luke (Luke-Acts) using it most frequently (twenty-eight times). By comparison, Mark and John use it only once each and Matthew not at all. In the epistles we might at first think that Paul is comfortable with the optative because throughout his letters it occurs thirty-one times, twelve times in Romans alone. Our confidence is diminished somewhat when we consider that nearly half (fourteen) of the Pauline uses are the static phrase μὴ γένοιτο.

In the New Testament the optative is mostly confined to wish and potential clauses. The following uses are attested.

A. Wishes

Meaning: The optative may be used to express a wish.
Identification: The optative will be the verb of an independent clause.

> *Examples:* χάρις ὑμῖν καὶ εἰρήνη πληθυνθείη. 1 Pet 1:2
> "*May* grace and peace *abound* to you!"

Optative Mood

ἐπιμένωμεν τῇ ἁμαρτίᾳ, ἵνα ἡ χάρις πλεονάσῃ; μὴ γένοιτο.
Rom 6:1-2

Shall we remain in sin so that grace may abound? *May it not be!*

B. Potential

Meaning: The optative may be used to express something that might, may, or could happen.
Identification: The optative with ἄν will be the verb of an independent clause.

> *Example:* πῶς γὰρ ἂν δυναίμην ἐὰν μή τις ὁδηγήσει με;
> Acts 8:31
> "For how *could I (might I be able)* unless someone guides me?"

C. Future Less Vivid Formulas

Meaning: A condition or other statement that is somewhat remote in the mind of the speaker. No complete example is found in the New Testament.
Identification: εἰ + optative in the protasis, optative + ἄν in the apodosis.

> *Example:* κρεῖττον γὰρ ἀγαθοποιοῦντας, εἰ θέλοι τὸ θέλημα τοῦ θεοῦ, πάσχειν ἢ κακοποιοῦντας. 1 Pet 3:17
> "If it *should be* the will of God, it *would be* better to suffer for doing good than for doing evil."

D. Dependent Clauses in Secondary Sequence

Meaning: When the verb of the independent clause is a secondary tense (imperfect, aorist, pluperfect), for stylistic reasons in Classical Greek the optative regularly takes the place of an original indicative or subjunctive in various attached dependent clauses such as indirect questions, indirect statements, fear clauses, etc. However, this happens only a few times in the New Testament, all of them in Luke.
Identification: The optative is found in an indirect statement or question after a secondary tense main verb.

Examples: διελογίζετο ποταπὸς εἴη ὁ ἀσπασμὸς οὗτος. Luke 1:29

"She was wondering what sort of greeting this was."

ἐπηρώτων δὲ αὐτὸν οἱ μαθηταὶ αὐτοῦ τίς αὕτη εἴη ἡ παραβολή. Luke 8:9

"His disciples began to ask him what this parable meant."

9

Infinitive

The infinitive is a verbal noun and in English is easily recognized as a verb with "to" preceding it such as "to sing, to laugh, to walk, to think." Like a noun it can be the subject or object of a sentence. An example in English would be "I love to sing," where "to sing" is the direct object of the verb "love." Like a verb, the infinitive may itself take various objects and modifiers. In the sentence "I love to sing hymns loudly," the infinitive "to sing" has both a direct object (hymns) and an adverb (loudly).

Greek infinitives share many of these same characteristics. Like nouns, Greek infinitives will often take an article, always in the neuter, and the article will further define how the infinitive functions in a sentence. Moreover, Greek infinitives will often follow prepositions and in this way express a variety of dependent clauses. When the infinitive itself has a subject, that subject will always be in the accusative case unless it is the same as the subject of the main clause.

A. Without the Article

1. Subject of a sentence

The simple infinitive may be used as the subject of a sentence.

> οὕτως γὰρ πρέπον ἐστὶν ἡμῖν πληρῶσαι πᾶσαν δικαιοσύνην. Matt 3:15
> For it is fitting for us in this way *to fulfill* all righteousness.

Often, however, the infinitive is part of a noun clause. In this case, the entire clause functions as the subject of a sentence and an accusative subject of the infinitive will often be present. Note the following examples:

> ἔδει δὲ αὐτὸν διέρχεσθαι διὰ τῆς Σαμαρείας. John 4:4
> "Now it was necessary *that he pass through Samaria.*" (Literally, "Him passing though Samaria was necessary.")

> μετὰ ταῦτα δεῖ λυθῆναι αὐτὸν μικρὸν χρόνον. Rev 20:3
> "Afterwards, it is necessary *that he be freed for a little while.*" (Literally, "Him being set free a short time is necessary.")

2. Indirect Statements and Reported Speech

The infinitive is regularly used to present a noun clause in reported speech or indirect statements. The subject of the infinitive, if different from the main verb, is placed in the accusative case. This type of construction typically follows verbs of saying, thinking, or believing.

> καὶ αὐτὸς ἐπηρώτα αὐτούς· ὑμεῖς δὲ τίνα με λέγετε εἶναι; Mark 8:29
> "And he himself was questioning them, 'But who do you yourselves say *that I am.*'"

> καὶ ἔρχονται Σαδδουκαῖοι πρὸς αὐτόν, οἵτινες λέγουσιν ἀνάστασιν μὴ εἶναι. Mark 12:18
> "And Sadducees came to him, who say *that there is no resurrection.*"

3. Complementary

The infinitive follows verbs or adjectives expressing fitness, ability, capacity, and the like to complete the idea.

> σκάπτειν οὐκ ἰσχύω, ἐπαιτεῖν αἰσχύνομαι. Luke 16:3
> "I am not strong enough *to dig*, I am too ashamed *to beg.*"

οὗ οὐκ εἰμὶ ἱκανὸς κύψας λῦσαι τὸν ἱμάντα τῶν ὑποδημάτων αὐτοῦ. Mark 1:7
"I am not worthy to stoop and *untie* the thongs of his sandals."

4. Imperative

The infinitive may occasionally be used to express a command.

πλὴν εἰς ὃ ἐφθάσαμεν, τῷ αὐτῷ στοιχεῖν. Phil 3:16
"However, to that which we have attained, *keep in line* with the same!"

5. Purpose

μὴ νομίσητε ὅτι ἦλθον καταλῦσαι τὸν νόμον ἢ τοὺς προφήτας. Matt 5:17
"Do not think that I came *to destroy (for the purpose of destroying)* the law and the prophets!"

6. Result

The infinitive may follow ὥστε to express a result and is often best translated as "so as" or "so that." ὥστε may also be followed by an indicative to stress the fact of the result. Care must be taken not to confuse result with purpose. The two are often related yet are distinct.

ἔδωκεν αὐτοῖς ἐξουσίαν πνευμάτων ἀκαθάρτων ὥστε ἐκβάλλειν αὐτά. Matt 10:1
"He gave them authority over unclean spirits *so that they cast them out (with the result that they cast them out)*."

B. With the Article

1. With τό as subject or object.

ἔκρινα γὰρ ἐμαυτῷ τοῦτο τὸ μὴ πάλιν ἐν λύπῃ πρὸς ὑμᾶς ἐλθεῖν. 2 Cor 2:1

"For I decided this for myself, *not to come* again to you in pain."

2. With τοῦ.

a. Purpose

μέλλει γὰρ Ἡρῴδης ζητεῖν τὸ παιδίον τοῦ ἀπολέσαι αὐτό. Matt 2:13

"For Herod intends to seek the child *in order to destroy* it."

b. Result

ὑμεῖς δὲ ἰδόντες οὐδὲ μετεμελήθητε ὕστερον τοῦ πιστεῦσαι αὐτῷ. Matt 21:32

"But after you yourselves saw (this), you did not even repent later *so that (with the result that)* you believed in him."

c. Complementary

πάλιν χρείαν ἔχετε τοῦ διδάσκειν ὑμᾶς τινὰ τὰ στοιχεῖα. Heb 5:12

"You again have a need for someone *to teach* you the elementary principles."

Infinitive

3. With τῷ to express cause, manner, or means.

οὐκ ἔσχηκα ἄνεσιν τῷ πνεύματί μου τῷ μὴ εὑρεῖν με Τίτον τὸν ἀδελφόν μου. 2 Cor 2:13
"I had no rest in my spirit because I did not find Titus, my brother."

C. Prepositions with the Articular Infinitive

As a verbal noun, the infinitive with the article may follow a variety of prepositions and thus it becomes a common way to express many dependent clauses. How the infinitive should be translated can usually be inferred from the preposition and the case of the infinitive. The following is a representative list.

διὰ τὸ βλέπειν αὐτόν = cause ("because he sees")

εἰς τὸ βλέπειν αὐτόν = purpose ("in order that he sees") or result ("so that he sees")

μετὰ τὸ βλέπειν αὐτόν = temporal ("after he sees")

πρὸς τὸ βλέπειν αὐτόν = purpose ("in order that he sees")

ἐν τῷ βλέπειν αὐτόν = temporal ("while/when he sees") or means ("by his seeing")

πρὸ τοῦ βλέπειν αὐτόν = temporal ("before he sees")

When an infinitive is used in this way to express a dependent clause, the subject of the infinitive, if different from the subject of the main verb, is always placed in the accusative case. Note also that in such constructions the tense of the infinitive often has temporal significance. See the related material above under "Tenses in Indirect Statements."

Examples:

καὶ διὰ τὸ μὴ ἔχειν ῥίζαν ἐξηράνθη. Mark 4:6
"And *because it had* no root, it withered."

ἀλλὰ μετὰ τὸ ἐγερθῆναί με προάξω ὑμᾶς εἰς τὴν Γαλιλαίαν. Mark 14:28

"But *after I am raised*, I will go before you into Galilee."

προσέχετε δὲ τὴν δικαιοσύνην ὑμῶν μὴ ποιεῖν ἔμπροσθεν τῶν ἀνθρώπων πρὸς τὸ θεαθῆναι αὐτοῖς. Matt 6:1

"But be careful not to carry out your righteousness before people *in order to be seen* by them!"

πρὸ τοῦ δὲ ἐλθεῖν τὴν πίστιν ὑπὸ νόμον ἐφρουρούμεθα. Gal 3:23

"But *before faith came*, we were held prisoner under the law."

καὶ ἐγένετο ἐν τῷ εὐλογεῖν αὐτὸν αὐτοὺς διέστη ἀπ' αὐτῶν. Luke 24:51

"And it happened that *while he was blessing* them, he went away from them."

10

Imperatives and Prohibitions

The imperative mood at heart expresses strong desire and intention and is, therefore, the mood often used to express commands and entreaties.

A. Direct Command

τῷ αἰτοῦντί σε δός. Matt 5:42
"*Give* to the one who asks you (for something)!"

εἰ δέ τις ὑμῶν λείπεται σοφίας, αἰτείτω παρὰ τοῦ διδόντος θεοῦ πᾶσιν ἁπλῶς καὶ μὴ ὀνειδίζοντος. Jas 1:5
"If one of you is lacking wisdom, *let him ask* (for it) from God, who gives to all sincerely and without reproach!"

B. Entreaty

When the imperative mood is directed towards a superior, its force is more akin to a polite request or entreaty. This is the normal way of addressing God in prayer.

ἀλλ' εἴ τι δύνῃ, βοήθησον ἡμῖν. Mark 9:22
"But if you are in any way able, *help* us!"

τὸν ἄρτον ἡμῶν τὸν ἐπιούσιον δίδου ἡμῖν τὸ καθ' ἡμέραν.
Luke 11:3

"*Give* us today our bread sufficient for the day!"

C. Prohibitions

The present imperative is used with μή to forbid a continuous activity and is therefore often used to forbid an activity that is already in progress. In such cases the prohibition is often best translated as "stop. . .."

μὴ ποιεῖτε τὸν οἶκον τοῦ πατρός μου οἶκον ἐμπορίου. John 2:16
"*Stop making* my father's house a marketplace!"

μή μου ἅπτου, οὔπω γὰρ ἀναβέβηκα πρὸς τὸν πατέρα.
John 20:17
"*Stop clinging* to me, for I have not yet ascended to the father!"

The aorist subjunctive is used with μή to forbid an activity without any reference to its frequency or progress. It is generally used to forbid an activity that has not yet begun.

μὴ κτήσησθε χρυσὸν μηδὲ ἄργυρον μηδὲ χαλκὸν εἰς τὰς ζώνας ὑμῶν. Matt 10:9
"*Do not acquire* money for your wallets!"

11

Participles

A participle is a verbal adjective. Like a verb, it may have direct objects and adverbs. Like an adjective, it always modifies a noun or pronoun, agreeing with it in number, gender, and case. There are five main uses of the participle.

A. Attributive

Meaning: The participle is used like an adjective. It is often best translated by means of a relative clause.

Identification: The participle is placed in the attributive position with a noun or pronoun. That is, besides agreeing with the noun/pronoun in number, gender, and case, the participle will be preceded by an article. The participle with an article might also be found as a substantive.

> *Examples:* ἴδε ὁ ἀμνὸς τοῦ θεοῦ ὁ αἴρων τὴν ἁμαρτίαν τοῦ κόσμου. John 1:29
> "Behold the lamb of God, *who takes away* the sin of the world."
>
> ὁ ἔχων τὰς ἐντολάς μου καὶ τηρῶν αὐτὰς ἐκεῖνός ἐστιν ὁ ἀγαπῶν με. John 14:21
> "*He who has* my commandments *and keeps* them, that is *the one who loves* me."

B. Predicate

Meaning: The participle sets forth the circumstances of the main verb. Greek authors used the predicate participle as a short hand way to express a variety of dependent/adverbial clauses. The translator must examine the context in deciding exactly which type of adverbial clause to use in translation. Note the following:

>Time: "When, while, after. . ."
>
>Cause: "Because. . ."
>
>Manner: "— -ing. . ."
>
>Means: "By — -ing. . ."
>
>Condition: "If. . ."
>
>Concession: "Although. . ."
>
>Purpose: "In order to. . ."
>
>Attendant Circumstance: Participle translated as indicative, joined by "and"

Identification: The participle stands in the predicate position and generally agrees with the subject or object.

>*Examples:* καὶ εὐθὺς ἐκ τῆς συναγωγῆς ἐξελθόντες ἦλθον εἰς τὴν οἰκίαν. Mark 1:29
>"And immediately *after they left* the synagogue, they came into the house."
>
>καὶ ἦλθεν κηρύσσων εἰς τὰς συναγωγὰς αὐτῶν. Mark 1:39
>"And he came into their synagogues, *preaching.*"

C. Supplementary

Meaning: The participle completes the meaning of certain verbs.
Identification: The participle is linked with verbs like "begin, cease, endure, grow weary." In this construction the participle is frequently found in the New Testament with εἰμί (the "periphrastic" use).

Participles

Examples: τὸ δὲ καλὸν ποιοῦντες μὴ ἐγκακῶμεν. Gal 6:9
"Let us not grow weary *doing* what is good."

καὶ ἐγενόμην νεκρὸς καὶ ἰδοὺ ζῶν εἰμι εἰς τοὺς αἰῶνας τῶν αἰώνων. Rev 1:18
"I was dead and behold *I live* forever."

D. Noun Clause

Meaning: A participle and noun in the accusative case may function as a noun clause.
Identification: The accusative noun and participle typically follow verbs of sense perception or mental activity (hearing, seeing, knowing, or showing).

Example: καὶ τότε ὄψονται τὸν υἱὸν τοῦ ἀνθρώπου ἐρχόμενον ἐν νεφέλαις μετὰ δυνάμεως πολλῆς καὶ δόξης. Mark 13:26
"And then they will see the son of man *coming* in the clouds with great power and glory."

E. Genitive Absolute

Meaning: Commonly translated as a temporal clause, though strictly speaking it might also be translated as any of the adverbial clauses listed above.
Identification: Genitive noun or pronoun with a genitive participle.

Example: ταῦτα αὐτοῦ λαλοῦντος πολλοὶ ἐπίστευσαν εἰς αὐτόν. John 8:30

"*After he said this,* many believed in him."
"*Because he said this,* many believed in him."

F. Tenses of the Participle

Tense aspect is always primary in the meaning of participles. See the discussion above under "Tenses of the Verb." However, when participles are expanded into clauses, care must be taken to do so relative to the time of the main verb. In such cases, the present participle denotes time *contemporaneous* with the main verb whereas an aorist participle denotes time *prior* to the main verb. A present participle, for example, when expanded into a finite verb, ought to be translated by means of the present tense if the main verb is in the present, but by means of the imperfect if the main verb is a secondary tense. Note the following examples.

ὁ διδάκαλος ἀκούει τοὺς μαθητὰς ἐκβαίνοντας ἐκ τῆς πόλεως.
"The teacher hears that his disciples *are leaving* the city."

ὁ διδάκαλος ἤκουσε τοὺς μαθητὰς ἐκβαίνοντας ἐκ τῆς πόλεως.
"The teacher heard that his disciples *were leaving* the city."

ὁ διδάκαλος ἀκούει τοὺς μαθητὰς ἐκβησόμενους ἐκ τῆς πόλεως.
"The teacher hears that his disciples *will leave* the city."

ὁ διδάκαλος ἤκουσε τοὺς μαθητὰς ἐκβησόμενους ἐκ τῆς πόλεως.
"The teacher heard that his disciples *would leave* the city."

ὁ διδάκαλος ἀκούει τοὺς μαθητὰς ἐκβάντας ἐκ τῆς πόλεως.
"The teacher hears that his disciples *left* the city."

ὁ διδάκαλος ἤκουσε τοὺς μαθητὰς ἐκβάντας ἐκ τῆς πόλεως.
"The teacher heard that his disciples *had left* the city."

12

Conditional Statements

A simple conditional statement is composed of two clauses as illustrated by the following example:

"If the master teaches, his disciples listen."

The *protasis*, also called the "if" clause, is the dependent clause while the *apodosis*, also called the "then" clause, is an independent clause. The New Testament authors, as authors in Classical and Hellenistic Greek, expressed conditional statements in a variety of ways to convey the nuance of the statement. We follow the labels here in keeping with standard introductions of Classical Greek but include also those common in New Testament grammars.

A. Simple Conditions (First Class Conditions)

Meaning: A statement assumed to be and expressed to make a point in discourse.
Identification: εἰ + indicative, any mood.

> *Example:* εἰ γὰρ κατὰ σάρκα ζῆτε, μέλλετε ἀποθνῄσκειν· εἰ δὲ πνεύματι τὰς πράξεις τοῦ σώματος θανατοῦτε, ζήσεσθε. Rom 8:13
>
> "For if you live in accordance with the flesh, you are about to die. But if you put to death the deeds of the body, you will live."

B. Future More Vivid (Third Class Conditions)

Meaning: A hypothetical statement about the future that is vivid in the mind of the speaker.
Identification: ἐάν + subjunctive, future indicative.

> *Example:* ἐὰν ἀγαπᾶτέ με, τὰς ἐντολὰς τὰς ἐμὰς τηρήσετε. John 14:15
> "If you love me, you will keep my commandments."

C. Future Less Vivid (Fourth Class Conditions)

Meaning: A hypothetical statement about the future that is somewhat remote in the mind of the speaker. No complete example is found in the New Testament.
Identification: εἰ + optative, optative + ἄν.

> *Example:* κρεῖττον γὰρ ἀγαθοποιοῦντας, εἰ θέλοι τὸ θέλημα τοῦ θεοῦ, πάσχειν ἢ κακοποιοῦντας. 1 Pet 3:17
> "If it *should be* the will of God, it *would be* better to suffer for doing good than for doing evil."

D. Present General (Third Class Conditions)

Meaning: A hypothetical statement about something that is generally assumed to be true at the time the statement is made.
Identification: ἐάν + subjunctive, present indicative.

> *Example:* ἐάν τις περιπατῇ ἐν τῇ ἡμέρᾳ, οὐ προσκόπτει. John 11:9
> "If (ever) someone walks during the day, he does not stumble."

E. Present Contrary to Fact (Second Class Conditions)

Meaning: A hypothetical statement that refers to present time but that is not fulfilled because it is contradicted by known fact.
Identification: εἰ + imperfect indicative, imperfect indicative + ἄν.

Conditional Statements

Example: εἰ γὰρ ἐπιστεύετε Μωϋσεῖ, ἐπιστεύετε ἂν ἐμοί.
John 5:46
"If you *were* believing in Moses, you *would* believe in me."
(But in fact you don't believe in Moses or me.)

F. Past Contrary to Fact (Second Class Conditions)

Meaning: A hypothetical statement that refers to past time but that was not fulfilled because it was contradicted by known fact.
Identification: εἰ + aorist indicative, aorist indicative + ἄν.

Example: κύριε, εἰ ἦς ὧδε οὐκ ἂν ἀπέθανεν ὁ ἀδελφός μου.
John 11:21
"Lord, if you *had been* here, my brother *would not have* died."
(But in fact you were not here, and my brother died.)

13

Uses of οὐ and μή

A. General Usage

οὐ negates direct statements and, therefore, just about always negates verbs in the indicative. By contrast, μή is used to negate hypothetical statements, wishes, and doubtful or indirect statements and is primarily used to negate all other moods.

B. Double Negatives

If the second of successive negatives is a compound negative, the negatives do not cancel each other as they would in English. Rather, they strengthen each other. In translation one of the negatives must be turned into a positive.

> οὐκ ἔφαγεν οὐδὲν ἐν ταῖς ἡμέραις ἐκείναις. Luke 4:2
> "He ate nothing in those days."

C. In Questions

1. οὐ often introduces a question which expects a "yes" answer.

> οὐχ οὗτός ἐστιν ὁ τοῦ τέκτονος υἱός; Matt 13:55
> "He is the carpenter's son, isn't he?"

οὐχὶ ταῦτα ἔδει παθεῖν τὸν χριστὸν καὶ εἰσελθεῖν εἰς τὴν δόξαν αὐτοῦ; Luke 24:26
"The Messiah did have to suffer and enter his glory in this manner, didn't he?"

2. μή often introduces a question which expects a "no" answer.

μὴ σὺ μείζων εἶ τοῦ πατρὸς ἡμῶν Ἰακώβ; John 4:12
"You aren't greater than our father Jacob, are you?"

μὴ πάντες γλώσσαις λαλοῦσιν; 1 Cor 12:30
"All do not speak in tongues, do they?"

D. Emphatic Negative

οὐ and μή are used together with the aorist subjunctive or less often with the future indicative in an emphatic denial. This is in fact the strongest negative employed in New Testament Greek.

καὶ πᾶς ὁ ζῶν καὶ πιστεύων εἰς ἐμὲ οὐ μὴ ἀποθάνῃ εἰς τὸν αἰῶνα. John 11:26
"Each one who lives and believes in me will *certainly* never die."

14

Aramaic Constructions

New Testament Greek often shows the influence of Hebrew and Aramaic, resulting in constructions that, while evidenced in the Septuagint and other Jewish Greek writings, are not found in Classical or Hellenistic Greek. Besides the Genitive of Definition and Genitive of Apposition already mentioned above, it might be argued that some of the ἵνα constructions (as subject, object, or in apposition) fall under this category. Additionally, the following should be noted.

A. καὶ ἐγένετο (ἐγένετο δέ)

Exhibited in Luke's writings, this construction reflects the Septuagint, where it is the equivalent of וַיְהִי ("and it came to pass"), which is regularly used merely to introduce narration in past time and is often best left untranslated.

> ἐγένετο δὲ ἐν ταῖς ἡμέραις ἐκείναις ἐξῆλθεν δόγμα παρὰ Καίσαρος Αὐγούστου. Luke 2:1
> "(And it came to pass) in those days (that) a decree went out from Caesar Augustus."

B. καί

The prevalence and use of καί reflects the Hebrew and Aramaic conjunction וְ, which is used not only conjunctively but also disjunctively or to introduce a variety of dependent clauses. Note the following examples.

1. Disjunctive connector

τὸ φῶς ἐλήλυθεν εἰς τὸν κόσμον καὶ ἠγάπησαν οἱ ἄνθρωποι μᾶλλον τὸ σκότος ἢ τὸ φῶς. John 3:19
"The light has come into the world *and yet (but)* people loved darkness more than the light."

2. To introduce an apodosis

καὶ ὅτε ἐπλήσθησαν ἡμέραι ὀκτὼ τοῦ περιτεμεῖν αὐτὸν καὶ ἐκλήθη τὸ ὄνομα αὐτοῦ Ἰησοῦς. Luke 2:21
"And when the days were completed for him to be circumcised, he was named Jesus."

3. To introduce a coordinate temporal clause

ἦν δὲ ὥρα τρίτη καὶ ἐσταύρωσαν αὐτόν. Mark 15:25
"And it was the third hour *when* they crucified him."

C. ἰδού

The prevalence and use of ἰδού and ἰδέ ("behold") reflects the influence of the Septuagint, where the word translates הִנֵּה. The latter is used in Hebrew to point to the immediacy of something.

1. Existence or Prevalence

καὶ ἰδοὺ δύο τυφλοὶ καθήμενοι παρὰ τὴν ὁδόν. Matt 20:30
"And *there were* two blind men sitting beside the road."

2. To emphasize the whole or a part of a clause

ἰδοὺ ἡμεῖς ἀφήκαμεν πάντα καὶ ἠκολουθήκαμέν σοι. Mark 10:28
"*Look,* we ourselves have left everything and have followed you."

15

Translation and Composition Exercises

The following groupings of exercises emphasize various aspects of syntax though there is considerable overlap among all the sentences.

Turning sentences from English into Greek is increasingly a lost skill for those who learn New Testament Greek, but it has always been an important part of a Classics curriculum. There is perhaps no more thorough way to learn grammar and syntax than when one is forced to make choices when writing in Greek.

If you have never done this before, here are some suggestions to follow. For each sentence, first make a listing of the Greek words you will need. An English-to-Greek dictionary can be found at the back of this book to facilitate this process. Next decide how the words should be inflected. That is, what case should a noun take? What form should the verb take? Then in consultation with your basic Greek grammar book, construct your sentence.

Grammar Review—Emphasizing the Present Indicative

Translation: John 1:1–14

ἐν ἀρχῇ ἦν ὁ λόγος, καὶ ὁ λόγος ἦν πρὸς τὸν θεόν, καὶ θεὸς ἦν ὁ λόγος. [2] οὗτος ἦν ἐν ἀρχῇ πρὸς τὸν θεόν. [3] πάντα δι' αὐτοῦ ἐγένετο, καὶ χωρὶς αὐτοῦ ἐγένετο οὐδὲ ἕν. ὃ γέγονεν [4] ἐν αὐτῷ ζωὴ ἦν, καὶ ἡ ζωὴ ἦν τὸ φῶς τῶν ἀνθρώπων· [5] καὶ τὸ φῶς ἐν τῇ σκοτίᾳ[1] φαίνει, καὶ ἡ σκοτία αὐτὸ οὐ κατέλαβεν[2].

⁶ ἐγένετο ἄνθρωπος, ἀπεσταλμένος παρὰ θεοῦ, ὄνομα αὐτῷ Ἰωάννης· ⁷ οὗτος ἦλθεν εἰς μαρτυρίαν ἵνα μαρτυρήσῃ περὶ τοῦ φωτός, ἵνα πάντες πιστεύσωσιν δι' αὐτοῦ. ⁸ οὐκ ἦν ἐκεῖνος τὸ φῶς, ἀλλ' ἵνα μαρτυρήσῃ περὶ τοῦ φωτός. ⁹ ἦν τὸ φῶς τὸ ἀληθινόν,³ ὃ φωτίζει⁴ πάντα ἄνθρωπον, ἐρχόμενον εἰς τὸν κόσμον. ¹⁰ ἐν τῷ κόσμῳ ἦν, καὶ ὁ κόσμος δι' αὐτοῦ ἐγένετο, καὶ ὁ κόσμος αὐτὸν οὐκ ἔγνω. ¹¹ εἰς τὰ ἴδια ἦλθεν, καὶ οἱ ἴδιοι αὐτὸν οὐ παρέλαβον. ¹² ὅσοι δὲ ἔλαβον αὐτόν, ἔδωκεν αὐτοῖς ἐξουσίαν τέκνα θεοῦ γενέσθαι, τοῖς πιστεύουσιν εἰς τὸ ὄνομα αὐτοῦ, ¹³ οἳ οὐκ ἐξ αἱμάτων οὐδὲ ἐκ θελήματος σαρκὸς οὐδὲ ἐκ θελήματος ἀνδρὸς ἀλλ' ἐκ θεοῦ ἐγεννήθησαν.

¹⁴ καὶ ὁ λόγος σὰρξ ἐγένετο καὶ ἐσκήνωσεν⁵ ἐν ἡμῖν, καὶ ἐθεασάμεθα⁶ τὴν δόξαν αὐτοῦ, δόξαν ὡς μονογενοῦς παρὰ πατρός, πλήρης χάριτος καὶ ἀληθείας. (John 1:1–14)

---

¹*σκοτία -ας, ἡ*, darkness. ²*καταλαμβάνω*, obtain, overtake, seize. ³*ἀληθινός -η -ον*, true. ⁴*φωτίζω*, shine, illuminate. ⁵*σκηνόω*, dwell in a tent, tabernacle. ⁶*θεάομαι*, look at, see.

Translation and Composition Exercises

Composition

1. The prophet knows the disciples of God and brings them into the church.

2. The men teach the children of the Lord in the city.

3. The words are being spoken to the world and the people believe them.

4. Servants and sons are speaking words of love and bringing the apostles gifts.

5. We do not write the laws of men but teach the commandments of God.

6. You are going into the city with your brother to hear the words of the teacher.

7. Does our brother know the Lord and does he wish to be baptized?

8. The evil man comes to destroy the church and does not practice the truth.

9. The people are amazed because the prophet is doing miracles.

10. We see the glory of God in the temple and desire to worship there.

Translation and Composition Exercises

Grammar Review: Emphasizing the Imperfect and Aorist Indicative

Translation: John 3:1-11

ἦν δὲ ἄνθρωπος ἐκ τῶν Φαρισαίων, Νικόδημος ὄνομα αὐτῷ, ἄρχων τῶν Ἰουδαίων· ² οὗτος ἦλθεν πρὸς αὐτὸν νυκτὸς καὶ εἶπεν αὐτῷ· ῥαββί, οἴδαμεν ὅτι ἀπὸ θεοῦ ἐλήλυθας διδάσκαλος· οὐδεὶς γὰρ δύναται ταῦτα τὰ σημεῖα ποιεῖν ἃ σὺ ποιεῖς, ἐὰν μὴ ᾖ ὁ θεὸς μετ' αὐτοῦ. ³ ἀπεκρίθη Ἰησοῦς καὶ εἶπεν αὐτῷ· ἀμὴν ἀμὴν λέγω σοι, ἐὰν μή τις γεννηθῇ ἄνωθεν,¹ οὐ δύναται ἰδεῖν τὴν βασιλείαν τοῦ θεοῦ. ⁴ λέγει πρὸς αὐτὸν Νικόδημος· πῶς δύναται ἄνθρωπος γεννηθῆναι γέρων² ὤν; μὴ δύναται εἰς τὴν κοιλίαν³ τῆς μητρὸς αὐτοῦ δεύτερον εἰσελθεῖν καὶ γεννηθῆναι; ⁵ ἀπεκρίθη Ἰησοῦς· ἀμὴν ἀμὴν λέγω σοι, ἐὰν μή τις γεννηθῇ ἐξ ὕδατος καὶ πνεύματος, οὐ δύναται εἰσελθεῖν εἰς τὴν βασιλείαν τοῦ θεοῦ. ⁶ τὸ γεγεννημένον ἐκ τῆς σαρκὸς σάρξ ἐστιν, καὶ τὸ γεγεννημένον ἐκ τοῦ πνεύματος πνεῦμά ἐστιν. ⁷ μὴ θαυμάσῃς ὅτι εἶπόν σοι· δεῖ ὑμᾶς γεννηθῆναι ἄνωθεν.¹ ⁸ τὸ πνεῦμα ὅπου θέλει πνεῖ⁴ καὶ τὴν φωνὴν αὐτοῦ ἀκούεις, ἀλλ' οὐκ οἶδας πόθεν⁵ ἔρχεται καὶ ποῦ ὑπάγει· οὕτως ἐστὶν πᾶς ὁ γεγεννημένος ἐκ τοῦ πνεύματος. ⁹ ἀπεκρίθη Νικόδημος καὶ εἶπεν αὐτῷ· πῶς δύναται ταῦτα γενέσθαι; ¹⁰ ἀπεκρίθη Ἰησοῦς καὶ εἶπεν αὐτῷ· σὺ εἶ ὁ διδάσκαλος τοῦ Ἰσραὴλ καὶ ταῦτα οὐ γινώσκεις; ¹¹ ἀμὴν ἀμὴν λέγω σοι ὅτι ὃ οἴδαμεν λαλοῦμεν καὶ ὃ ἑωράκαμεν μαρτυροῦμεν, καὶ τὴν μαρτυρίαν ἡμῶν οὐ λαμβάνετε.

---

¹ἄνωθεν, *from above; again.* ²γέρων -οντος ὁ, *old man.* ³κοιλία -ας ἡ, *belly, womb.* ⁴πνέω, *blow, breath.* ⁵ποθεν, *from where.*

Composition

1. The Holy Spirit came down from heaven and gave power to the disciples.

2. The scribes taught the word of God to the people in the synagogue.

3. The prophet was sending the servants into the small house.

4. The sons of the prophets gathered the saints together in the temple.

5. I took the bread from the house to the church in the city.

Translation and Composition Exercises

6. The disciples sent letters to the churches of Christ and encouraged them to be strong.

7. You were seeing the works of God and on account of these things believed the gospel.

8. Righteousness from God came through Jesus because God loves all people.

9. The righteous master was leading his servants to the temple of God.

10. The apostles were teaching the people in the synagogues.

A Short New Testament Syntax

Grammar Review: Emphasizing Strong Verbs

Translation: John 3:12–21

¹² εἰ τὰ ἐπίγεια[1] εἶπον ὑμῖν καὶ οὐ πιστεύετε, πῶς ἐὰν εἴπω ὑμῖν τὰ ἐπουράνια[2] πιστεύσετε; ¹³ καὶ οὐδεὶς ἀναβέβηκεν εἰς τὸν οὐρανὸν εἰ μὴ ὁ ἐκ τοῦ οὐρανοῦ καταβάς, ὁ υἱὸς τοῦ ἀνθρώπου. ¹⁴ καὶ καθὼς Μωϋσῆς ὕψωσεν[3] τὸν ὄφιν[4] ἐν τῇ ἐρήμῳ, οὕτως ὑψωθῆναι[3] δεῖ τὸν υἱὸν τοῦ ἀνθρώπου, ¹⁵ ἵνα πᾶς ὁ πιστεύων ἐν αὐτῷ ἔχῃ ζωὴν αἰώνιον.

¹⁶ οὕτως γὰρ ἠγάπησεν ὁ θεὸς τὸν κόσμον, ὥστε τὸν υἱὸν τὸν μονογενῆ[5] ἔδωκεν, ἵνα πᾶς ὁ πιστεύων εἰς αὐτὸν μὴ ἀπόληται ἀλλ' ἔχῃ ζωὴν αἰώνιον. ¹⁷ οὐ γὰρ ἀπέστειλεν ὁ θεὸς τὸν υἱὸν εἰς τὸν κόσμον ἵνα κρίνῃ τὸν κόσμον, ἀλλ' ἵνα σωθῇ ὁ κόσμος δι' αὐτοῦ. ¹⁸ ὁ πιστεύων εἰς αὐτὸν οὐ κρίνεται· ὁ δὲ μὴ πιστεύων ἤδη κέκριται, ὅτι μὴ πεπίστευκεν εἰς τὸ ὄνομα τοῦ μονογενοῦς υἱοῦ τοῦ θεοῦ. ¹⁹ αὕτη δέ ἐστιν ἡ κρίσις ὅτι τὸ φῶς ἐλήλυθεν εἰς τὸν κόσμον καὶ ἠγάπησαν οἱ ἄνθρωποι μᾶλλον τὸ σκότος ἢ τὸ φῶς· ἦν γὰρ αὐτῶν πονηρὰ τὰ ἔργα. ²⁰ πᾶς γὰρ ὁ φαῦλα πράσσων μισεῖ τὸ φῶς καὶ οὐκ ἔρχεται πρὸς τὸ φῶς, ἵνα μὴ ἐλεγχθῇ τὰ ἔργα αὐτοῦ· ²¹ ὁ δὲ ποιῶν τὴν ἀλήθειαν ἔρχεται πρὸς τὸ φῶς, ἵνα φανερωθῇ αὐτοῦ τὰ ἔργα ὅτι ἐν θεῷ ἐστιν εἰργασμένα.

---

[1]ἐπίγειος -ον, *earthly*. [2]ἐπουράνιος -ον, *heavenly*. [3]ὑψόω, *lift up*. [4]ὄφις -εως, ἡ, *snake*. [5]μονογενής -ες, *only begotten*.

Translation and Composition Exercises

Composition

1. The righteous teacher was led by the scribe into the Lord's temple.

2. The apostles will carry the book from the wicked city and give it to the saints.

3. The crowds saw the Christ but they cried out against him.

4. Christ has been raised from the dead and will come again in great honor.

5. We were taught the way of righteousness and were baptized in the name of God.

6. In those days we led our children out of the house to see the trees at the river.

7. I will come to the city and I will carry fruit to the marketplace.

8. You (pl.) have spoken the word of God to the nations and they have known the truth.

9. The disciples brought the blind man into the church and he has heard the gospel.

10. The master died on a cross and we will now find forgiveness of our sins.

Translation and Composition Exercises

Noun Cases

Translation: John 4:7-15

⁷ ἔρχεται γυνὴ ἐκ τῆς Σαμαρείας ἀντλῆσαι[1] ὕδωρ. λέγει αὐτῇ ὁ Ἰησοῦς· δός μοι πεῖν· ⁸ οἱ γὰρ μαθηταὶ αὐτοῦ ἀπεληλύθεισαν εἰς τὴν πόλιν ἵνα τροφὰς ἀγοράσωσιν.[2] ⁹ λέγει οὖν αὐτῷ ἡ γυνὴ ἡ Σαμαρῖτις· πῶς σὺ Ἰουδαῖος ὢν παρ' ἐμοῦ πεῖν αἰτεῖς γυναικὸς Σαμαρίτιδος οὔσης; οὐ γὰρ συγχρῶνται[3] Ἰουδαῖοι Σαμαρίταις. ¹⁰ ἀπεκρίθη Ἰησοῦς καὶ εἶπεν αὐτῇ· εἰ ᾔδεις τὴν δωρεὰν[4] τοῦ θεοῦ καὶ τίς ἐστιν ὁ λέγων σοι· δός μοι πεῖν, σὺ ἂν ᾔτησας αὐτὸν καὶ ἔδωκεν ἄν σοι ὕδωρ ζῶν. ¹¹ λέγει αὐτῷ ἡ γυνή· κύριε, οὔτε ἄντλημα[5] ἔχεις καὶ τὸ φρέαρ[6] ἐστὶν βαθύ·[7] πόθεν[8] οὖν ἔχεις τὸ ὕδωρ τὸ ζῶν; ¹² μὴ σὺ μείζων εἶ τοῦ πατρὸς ἡμῶν Ἰακώβ, ὃς ἔδωκεν ἡμῖν τὸ φρέαρ[6] καὶ αὐτὸς ἐξ αὐτοῦ ἔπιεν καὶ οἱ υἱοὶ αὐτοῦ καὶ τὰ θρέμματα αὐτοῦ; ¹³ ἀπεκρίθη Ἰησοῦς καὶ εἶπεν αὐτῇ· πᾶς ὁ πίνων ἐκ τοῦ ὕδατος τούτου διψήσει[10] πάλιν· ¹⁴ ὃς δ' ἂν πίῃ ἐκ τοῦ ὕδατος οὗ ἐγὼ δώσω αὐτῷ, οὐ μὴ διψήσει[10] εἰς τὸν αἰῶνα, ἀλλὰ τὸ ὕδωρ ὃ δώσω αὐτῷ γενήσεται ἐν αὐτῷ πηγὴ[11] ὕδατος ἁλλομένου[12] εἰς ζωὴν αἰώνιον. ¹⁵ λέγει πρὸς αὐτὸν ἡ γυνή· κύριε, δός μοι τοῦτο τὸ ὕδωρ, ἵνα μὴ διψῶ[10] μηδὲ διέρχωμαι ἐνθάδε ἀντλεῖν.[1]

---

[1]ἀντλέω, draw (a liquid). [2]ἀγοράζω, buy. [3]συγχράομαι, associate with. [4]δωρεά -ᾶς, ἡ, gift. [5]ἄντλημα -ατος, τό, bucket. [6]φρέαρ -ατος, τό, well. [7]βαθύς -εῖα -ύ, deep. [8]πόθεν, from where. [9]θρέμμα -ατος, τό, flocks. [10]διψάω, be thirsty. [11]πηγή -ῆς, ἡ, spring. [12]ἅλλομαι, bubble up. [13]ἐνθάδε, here.

Composition

These sentences are designed to help you review how the various noun cases might be translated.

1. O people of God, all men are saved by faith because Christ was raised from death on the third (use τρίτος) day.

2. The prophets taught the people many commandments, but they did not listen to these things.

3. For many days the messenger was comforting those who (use a relative pronoun) were baptized with the holy gospel.

4. Within the hour the soldier will release you from prison and will lead you with joy to your house.

5. Hope in Christ is better than honor from the world.

6. I am dead in regard to sin but I am alive in regard to the grace of God.

7. The men from the city went out at night to see the stars.

8. Many good gifts are mine from God through Christ.

9. The overseer taught the congregation many words from the scriptures.

10. The blind man was brought by the disciples to Jesus and this same man trusted in the love of God.

A Short New Testament Syntax

Verb Tenses and Voices

Translation: John 4:16–26

¹⁶ λέγει αὐτῇ· ὕπαγε φώνησον τὸν ἄνδρα σου καὶ ἐλθὲ ἐνθάδε.[1] ¹⁷ ἀπεκρίθη ἡ γυνὴ καὶ εἶπεν αὐτῷ· οὐκ ἔχω ἄνδρα. λέγει αὐτῇ ὁ Ἰησοῦς· καλῶς εἶπας ὅτι ἄνδρα οὐκ ἔχω· ¹⁸ πέντε γὰρ ἄνδρας ἔσχες καὶ νῦν ὃν ἔχεις οὐκ ἔστιν σου ἀνήρ· τοῦτο ἀληθὲς[2] εἴρηκας. ¹⁹ λέγει αὐτῷ ἡ γυνή· κύριε, θεωρῶ ὅτι προφήτης εἶ σύ. ²⁰ οἱ πατέρες ἡμῶν ἐν τῷ ὄρει τούτῳ προσεκύνησαν· καὶ ὑμεῖς λέγετε ὅτι ἐν Ἱεροσολύμοις ἐστὶν ὁ τόπος ὅπου προσκυνεῖν δεῖ. ²¹ λέγει αὐτῇ ὁ Ἰησοῦς· πίστευέ μοι, γύναι, ὅτι ἔρχεται ὥρα ὅτε οὔτε ἐν τῷ ὄρει τούτῳ οὔτε ἐν Ἱεροσολύμοις προσκυνήσετε τῷ πατρί. ²² ὑμεῖς προσκυνεῖτε ὃ οὐκ οἴδατε· ἡμεῖς προσκυνοῦμεν ὃ οἴδαμεν, ὅτι ἡ σωτηρία ἐκ τῶν Ἰουδαίων ἐστίν. ²³ ἀλλ' ἔρχεται ὥρα καὶ νῦν ἐστιν, ὅτε οἱ ἀληθινοὶ[3] προσκυνηταὶ[4] προσκυνήσουσιν τῷ πατρὶ ἐν πνεύματι καὶ ἀληθείᾳ· καὶ γὰρ ὁ πατὴρ τοιούτους ζητεῖ τοὺς προσκυνοῦντας αὐτόν. ²⁴ πνεῦμα ὁ θεός, καὶ τοὺς προσκυνοῦντας αὐτὸν ἐν πνεύματι καὶ ἀληθείᾳ δεῖ προσκυνεῖν. ²⁵ λέγει αὐτῷ ἡ γυνή· οἶδα ὅτι Μεσσίας ἔρχεται ὁ λεγόμενος χριστός· ὅταν ἔλθῃ ἐκεῖνος, ἀναγγελεῖ[5] ἡμῖν ἅπαντα. ²⁶ λέγει αὐτῇ ὁ Ἰησοῦς· ἐγώ εἰμι, ὁ λαλῶν σοι.

---

¹*ἐνθάδε*, here. ²*ἀληθής -ές*, true. ³*ἀληθινός -ή -ον*, true. ⁴*προσκυνητής -οῦ, ὁ*, worshipper. ⁵*ἀναγγέλλω*, proclaim.

Translation and Composition Exercises

Composition

Analyze the following sentences and place the verbs in the appropriate tense and voice.

1. The messenger used to go to the city on the Sabbath and there he prayed in the temple.

2. The people have heard the gospel and are willing to be baptized by the apostle

3. I tried to preach the gospel of the kingdom in the synagogue but the people started persecuting me.

4. The apostles have written the word of God and all the people in the church read their words.

5. Every year the elders proclaimed in their own language the commandments which they heard from the Son of God.

6. The men were being sent out of the city and were led to the river to be baptized.

7. These children were praying in the church and their words were heard by God.

8. You will be led out of your house and brought before the king.

9. Because they feared the enemy the servants ran from the city and fled into the country.

10. The servants of Christ worship God in spirit and in truth.

Translation and Composition Exercises

Subjunctive

Translation

1. ἡ δὲ ἡμέρα ἤγγικεν. ἀποθώμεθα οὖν τὰ ἔργα τοῦ σκότους, ἐνδυσώμεθα δὲ τὰ ὅπλα τοῦ φωτός. Rom 13:12

2. ὥστε ὁ νόμος παιδαγωγὸς ἡμῶν γέγονεν εἰς Χριστόν, ἵνα ἐκ πίστεως δικαιωθῶμεν. Gal 3:24

3. κατέχωμεν τὴν ὁμολογίαν τῆς ἐλπίδος ἀκλινῆ, πιστὸς γὰρ ὁ ἐπαγγειλάμενος. Heb 10:23

4. εἶπεν οὖν ὁ Ἰησοῦς πρὸς αὐτόν· ἐὰν μὴ σημεῖα καὶ τέρατα ἴδητε, οὐ μὴ πιστεύσητε. John 4:48

5. ὅταν λέγωσιν· εἰρήνη καὶ ἀσφάλεια, τότε αἰφνίδιος αὐτοῖς ἐφίσταται ὄλεθρος ὥσπερ ἡ ὠδὶν τῇ ἐν γαστρὶ ἐχούσῃ, καὶ οὐ μὴ ἐκφύγωσιν. 1 Thess 5:3

6. τεκνία, μὴ ἀγαπῶμεν λόγῳ μηδὲ τῇ γλώσσῃ ἀλλὰ ἐν ἔργῳ καὶ ἀληθείᾳ. 1John 3:18

7. τεκνία μου, ταῦτα γράφω ὑμῖν ἵνα μὴ ἁμάρτητε. καὶ ἐάν τις ἁμάρτῃ, παράκλητον ἔχομεν πρὸς τὸν πατέρα Ἰησοῦν Χριστὸν δίκαιον. 1 John 2:1

8. εἶπον οὖν πρὸς αὐτόν· τί ποιῶμεν ἵνα ἐργαζώμεθα τὰ ἔργα τοῦ θεοῦ; John 6:28

9. ὅτι αὕτη ἐστὶν ἡ ἀγγελία ἣν ἠκούσατε ἀπ' ἀρχῆς, ἵνα ἀγαπῶμεν ἀλλήλους. 1 John 3:11

10. τὸν υἱὸν αὐτοῦ τὸν μονογενῆ ἀπέσταλκεν ὁ θεὸς εἰς τὸν κόσμον ἵνα ζήσωμεν δι' αὐτοῦ. 1 John 4:9

Translation and Composition Exercises

Composition

Analyze the following sentences and use a subjunctive wherever it is appropriate. The italicized words will give you an indication.

1. *Let us teach* the disciples the Lord's commandments so that they may *proclaim* them to others.

2. You will *certainly not go* into the city *to see* the temple.

3. If you are *baptized* in the name of the Lord, you will be saved and will come into eternal life.

4. The apostles have written to us about the kingdom *so that we may have* God's righteousness.

5. *Let us go* into the city so that *we might see* the Lord in the temple.

6. *Do not bring* your son from the synagogue, for the disciple of Jesus is preaching there so that all the people *might have* faith in Christ.

7. If the soldiers *come* into the city *to speak* to us, *do not listen* to their words.

8. Do not fear those who kill the body but are unable to kill the soul.

9. Let us proclaim the good news to all the nations!

10. The Lord came so that sinners might have life.

Translation and Composition Exercises

Participles

Translation

1. ἰδὼν δὲ τοὺς ὄχλους ἀνέβη εἰς τὸ ὄρος, καὶ καθίσαντος αὐτοῦ προσῆλθαν αὐτῷ οἱ μαθηταὶ αὐτοῦ. Matt 5:1

2. ἔτι ἁμαρτωλῶν ὄντων ἡμῶν Χριστὸς ὑπὲρ ἡμῶν ἀπέθανεν. Rom 5:8

3. εἰ οὖν ὑμεῖς πονηροὶ ὄντες οἴδατε δόματα ἀγαθὰ διδόναι τοῖς τέκνοις ὑμῶν, πόσῳ μᾶλλον ὁ πατὴρ ὑμῶν ὁ ἐν τοῖς οὐρανοῖς δώσει ἀγαθὰ τοῖς αἰτοῦσιν αὐτόν. Matt 7:11

4. εἰ δέ τις ὑμῶν λείπεται σοφίας, αἰτείτω παρὰ τοῦ διδόντος θεοῦ πᾶσιν ἁπλῶς καὶ μὴ ὀνειδίζοντος καὶ δοθήσεται αὐτῷ. Jas 1:5

5. νυνὶ δὲ χωρὶς νόμου δικαιοσύνη θεοῦ πεφανέρωται μαρτυρουμένη ὑπὸ τοῦ νόμου καὶ τῶν προφητῶν, δικαιοσύνη δὲ θεοῦ διὰ πίστεως Ἰησοῦ Χριστοῦ εἰς πάντας τοὺς πιστεύοντας. Rom 3:21–22

6. ὁ νόμος παιδαγωγὸς ἡμῶν γέγονεν εἰς Χριστόν, ἵνα ἐκ πίστεως δικαιωθῶμεν· ἐλθούσης δὲ τῆς πίστεως οὐκέτι ὑπὸ παιδαγωγόν ἐσμεν. Gal 3:24-25

7. λήμψεσθε δύναμιν ἐπελθόντος τοῦ ἁγίου πνεύματος ἐφ' ὑμᾶς καὶ ἔσεσθέ μου μάρτυρες. Acts 1:8

8. ἔχοντες οὖν ἀρχιερέα μέγαν διεληλυθότα τοὺς οὐρανούς, Ἰησοῦν τὸν υἱὸν τοῦ θεοῦ, κρατῶμεν τῆς ὁμολογίας. Heb 4:14

9. ἐγώ εἰμι ὁ πρῶτος καὶ ὁ ἔσχατος καὶ ὁ ζῶν, καὶ ἐγενόμην νεκρὸς καὶ ἰδοὺ ζῶν εἰμι εἰς τοὺς αἰῶνας τῶν αἰώνων. Rev 1:17-18

Translation and Composition Exercises

Composition

Analyze the following sentences and use a participle wherever it is appropriate. The italicized words will give you an indication.

1. *Those who are being saved* by the Lord know those who *believe* God's word.

2. *While we were teaching* in the temple, we saw the one who *saves* us.

3. *When they had received* these gifts from *those who had brought* them, they came together in the church.

4. *As we were going* through the desert, we taught those who were with us.

5. *The men who heard* the apostle saw the house *that had been destroyed* by the soldiers.

6. *When our names have been written* in the book of life, we will see the Lord.

7. *Because the apostle had been thrown* into prison, the disciples went away from the city.

8. Although *the Pharisees had heard* the words of Jesus, many did not believe that he was from God.

9. A righteousness *that was testified* in the Law has come from God through faith in Jesus Christ.

10. I see that the disciples *are healing* the sick and *proclaiming* the grace of God in Jesus.

Translation and Composition Exercises

Infinitive

Translation

1. καὶ μὴ συσχηματίζεσθε τῷ αἰῶνι τούτῳ, ἀλλὰ μεταμορφοῦσθε τῇ ἀνακαινώσει τοῦ νοός εἰς τὸ δοκιμάζειν ὑμᾶς τί τὸ θέλημα τοῦ θεοῦ. Rom 12:2

2. ἔστω δὲ πᾶς ἄνθρωπος ταχὺς εἰς τὸ ἀκοῦσαι, βραδὺς εἰς τὸ λαλῆσαι, βραδὺς εἰς ὀργήν. Jas 1:19

3. ἐνδύσασθε τὴν πανοπλίαν τοῦ θεοῦ πρὸς τὸ δύνασθαι ὑμᾶς στῆναι πρὸς τὰς μεθοδείας τοῦ διαβόλου. Eph 6:11

4. ἐγένετο δὲ ἐν τῷ ἐγγίζειν αὐτὸν εἰς Ἰεριχὼ τυφλός τις ἐκάθητο παρὰ τὴν ὁδὸν ἐπαιτῶν. Luke 18:35

5. ὁ δὲ ἀποκριθεὶς εἶπεν· οὐκ ἔστιν καλὸν λαβεῖν τὸν ἄρτον τῶν τέκνων καὶ βαλεῖν τοῖς κυναρίοις. Matt 15:26

6. ἡμᾶς δεῖ ἐργάζεσθαι τὰ ἔργα τοῦ πέμψαντός με ἕως ἡμέρα ἐστίν· ἔρχεται νὺξ ὅτε οὐδεὶς δύναται ἐργάζεσθαι. John 9:4

7. τοὺς γὰρ πάντας ἡμᾶς φανερωθῆναι δεῖ ἔμπροσθεν τοῦ βήματος τοῦ Χριστοῦ. 2 Cor 5:10

8. λογιζόμεθα γὰρ δικαιοῦσθαι πίστει ἄνθρωπον χωρὶς ἔργων νόμου. Rom 3:28

9. μετὰ φόβου καὶ τρόμου τὴν ἑαυτῶν σωτηρίαν κατεργάζεσθε· θεὸς γάρ ἐστιν ὁ ἐνεργῶν ἐν ὑμῖν καὶ τὸ θέλειν καὶ τὸ ἐνεργεῖν ὑπὲρ τῆς εὐδοκίας. Phil 2:12–13

10. τί οὖν ἐροῦμεν εὑρηκέναι Ἀβραὰμ τὸν προπάτορα ἡμῶν κατὰ σάρκα; Rom 4:1

Translation and Composition Exercises

Composition

Analyze the following sentences and use the infinitive wherever it is appropriate. The italicized verbs in particular can all be expressed with the infinitive.

1. *When* the apostle *had been thrown* into prison, the disciples went away from the city. (Articular infinitive with preposition)

2. *Because* our names *have been written* in the book of life, we will see the Lord. (Articular infinitive with preposition)

3. I think that the disciple of Jesus *went* to the city.

4. The apostles of the Lord said that those who believe in Jesus *would be saved*.

5. The disciples left the church *because* God *had commanded* them *to go* into the desert.

6. The messengers came from the city *in order to proclaim* the words of the king.

7. I was not able *to speak* to the soldier who came to my house because I *had gone* to the temple.

8. God works in the disciples of Jesus both *to will* and *to do* His good pleasure.

9. The sick desired *to see* Jesus *in order to be healed*.

10. *Because* they *had been filled* with the Holy Spirit, the disciples were able *to proclaim* the gospel in power.

Translation and Composition Exercises

Conditional Statements

Translation

1. ἀμὴν λέγω ὑμῖν· ὅσα ἐὰν δήσητε ἐπὶ τῆς γῆς ἔσται δεδεμένα ἐν οὐρανῷ, καὶ ὅσα ἐὰν λύσητε ἐπὶ τῆς γῆς ἔσται λελυμένα ἐν οὐρανῷ. Matt 18:18

2. ἐὰν ὁμολογῶμεν τὰς ἁμαρτίας ἡμῶν, πιστός ἐστιν καὶ δίκαιος, ἵνα ἀφῇ ἡμῖν τὰς ἁμαρτίας καὶ καθαρίσῃ ἡμᾶς ἀπὸ πάσης ἀδικίας. 1 John 1:9

3. εἰ γὰρ ἐδόθη νόμος ὁ δυνάμενος ζῳοποιῆσαι, ὄντως ἐκ νόμου ἂν ἦν ἡ δικαιοσύνη. Gal 3:21

4. εἰ ἐκ τοῦ κόσμου τούτου ἦν ἡ βασιλεία ἡ ἐμή, οἱ ὑπηρέται οἱ ἐμοὶ ἠγωνίζοντο ἂν ἵνα μὴ παραδοθῶ τοῖς Ἰουδαίοις. John 18:36

5. οὗτος εἰ ἦν προφήτης, ἐγίνωσκεν ἂν τίς καὶ ποταπὴ ἡ γυνὴ ἥτις ἅπτεται αὐτοῦ, ὅτι ἁμαρτωλός ἐστιν. Luke 7:39

6. οὐδεὶς τῶν ἀρχόντων τοῦ αἰῶνος τούτου ἔγνωκεν· εἰ γὰρ ἔγνωσαν, οὐκ ἂν τὸν κύριον τῆς δόξης ἐσταύρωσαν. 1 Cor 2:8

7. ἀλλ' εἰ καὶ πάσχοιτε διὰ δικαιοσύνην, μακάριοι. 1 Pet 3:14

8. εἰ δὲ ἀπεθάνομεν σὺν Χριστῷ, πιστεύομεν ὅτι καὶ συζήσομεν αὐτῷ. Rom 6:8

9. εἰ δέ τις πνεῦμα Χριστοῦ οὐκ ἔχει, οὗτος οὐκ ἔστιν αὐτοῦ. Rom 8:9

10. ὅτι ἐὰν ὁμολογήσῃς ἐν τῷ στόματί σου κύριον Ἰησοῦν καὶ πιστεύσῃς ἐν τῇ καρδίᾳ σου ὅτι ὁ θεὸς αὐτὸν ἤγειρεν ἐκ νεκρῶν, σωθήσῃ. Rom 10:9

Translation and Composition Exercises

Composition

1. If the people had believed in the Messiah, they would have listened to his teaching.

2. If the disciples were having no hope, they would flee persecution.

3. If you confess your sins to God, He is faithful in Christ to forgive your sins.

4. If you love God, you will love the brothers.

5. When we come to the Lord's table, we receive his own body and blood for our salvation.

6. If you have been baptized, you have been united to the death and resurrection of Jesus.

7. Whoever believes that Jesus Christ is the Lord and trusts that God has raised him from the dead will be saved.

8. If you commit your ways to the Lord, he will give you the desires of your heart.

9. If you do not forgive the sins of others, your own sins are not forgiven.

10. If you had not seen the mighty works of God, you would not have turned from your ways.

Appendix

English to Greek Dictionary

Able (v) δύναμαι
Again πάλιν
Against ἐπί +acc.
All πᾶς, πᾶσα, πᾶν
Apostle ἀπόστολος –ου ὁ
Baptize βαπτίζω
Be εἰμί
Because ὅτι
Before ἐνώπιον, πρό +gen.
Believe πιστεύω
Better See Good
Blind τυφλός –η –ον
Blood αἷμα -ατος τό
Body σῶμα –ατος, τό
Book βιβλίον –ου τό
Bread ἄρτος –ου ὁ
Bring ἄγω; φέρω
Brother ἀδελφός –ου ὁ
But ἀλλά
By means of (use the dative case)
By ὑπό + gen.
Carry φέρω
Child τεκνίον –ου τό
Christ Χριστός –ου ὁ

Church ἐκκλησία –ας ἡ
City πόλις –εως ἡ
Come down κατέρχομαι
Come together συνάγω (mid)
Come ἔρχομαι
Comfort (v) παρακαλέω
Command v. κελεύω
Commandment ἐντολή -ῆς ἡ
Commit παρατίθημι
Confess ὁμολογέω
Congregation ἐκκλησία –ας, ἡ
Country ἀγρός –ου ὁ
Cross σταυρός –οῦ ὁ
Crowd ὄχλος –ου ὁ
Cry out κράζω
Day ἡμέρα –ας ἡ
Dead νεκρός –α –ον
Death θάνατος –ου ὁ
Deed ἔργον –ου τό
Desert ἔρημος –ου ὁ
Desire n. θέλημα –ατος τό
Desire v. θέλω
Destroy λύω
Die ἀποθνῄσκω

Disciple μαθητής –ου ὁ
Do ποιέω
Elder πρεσβύτερος –α –ον
Encourage παρακαλέω
Enemy πόλεμος –ου ὁ
Eternal αἰώνιος –α –ον
Every πᾶς, πᾶσα, πᾶν
Evil πονηρός –ά –όν
Faith πίστις –εως ἡ
Faithful πιστός –η –ον
Fear φοβέομαι
Fill πληρόω
Find εὑρίσκω
First πρῶτος –η –ον
Flee φεύγω
For ἐπεί, ὅτι
Forgive ἀφίημι
Forgiveness ἄφεσις –έως ἡ
From ἐκ; ἀπό
Fruit καρπός –οῦ ὁ
Gather / Gather together συνάγω
Gift δῶρον –ου τό
Give δίδωμι
Glory δόξα –ας ἡ
Go away ἐξέρχομαι; ἀπέρχομαι
Go through διέρχομαι
Go ἔρχομαι
God θεός –ου ὁ
Good News (see Gospel)
Good ἀγαθός –η –ον; καλός –η –ον
Gospel εὐαγγέλιον –ου τό
Grace χάρις –ιτος ἡ
Great μέγας, μεγάλη, μέγα
Greater μείζων –ονος
Have Faith See Believe
Have ἔχω
He αὐτός –η –ο
Heal ἰάομαι

Hear ἀκούω
Heart καρδία –ας ἡ
Heaven οὐρανός –οῦ ὁ
Holy ἅγιος –α –ον
Honor τίμη –ης ἡ
Hope ἐλπίς –ίδος ἡ
Hour ὥρα –ας ἡ
House οἶκος –ου ὁ
I ἐγώ
If εἰ; ἐάν
In ἐν + dat.
Into εἰς + acc.
It (See He)
Jesus Ἰήσους –ου ὁ
Joy χαρά –ᾶς ἡ
Kill ἀποκτείνω
King βασιλεύς –έως ὁ
Kingdom βασιλεία –ας ἡ
Know γινώσκω
Language γλῶσσα –ης ἡ
Law νόμος –ου ὁ
Lead ἄγω
Leave (see Go Away)
Letter ἐπιστολή –ῆς ἡ
Life ζωή –ης ἡ
Listen (to) ἀκούω
Live ζάω
Lord κύριος –ου ὁ
Love ἀγαπάω
Love ἀγάπη –ης ἡ
Man ἄνθρωπος –ου ὁ; ἀνήρ ἀνδρός ὁ
Many πολύς, πολλή, πολύ
Marketplace ἀγορά –ᾶς ἡ
Master κύριος –ου ὁ
Messenger ἄγγελος –ου ὁ
Messiah χριστός –ου ὁ
Mighty ἰσχυρός –ά –όν
Name ὄνομα –ατος τό

English to Greek Dictionary

Nation ἔθνος –ους τό
Night νύξ νυκτός ἡ
No Longer οὐκέτι
On Account of διά +acc
Other ἄλλος –η –ο; ἕτερος –α –ον
Overseer ἐπίσκοπος –ου ὁ
Own ἴδιος –α –ον
People λαός –οῦ ὁ See also Man
Persecute διώκω
Persecution διωγμός –οῦ ὁ
Person See Man
Pharisee φαρισαῖος –ου ὁ
Pleasure εὐδοκία –ας ἡ
Power δύναμις –εως ἡ
Practice ποιέω
Pray προςεύχομαι
Preach κηρύσσω
Prison φυλακή -ῆς ἡ
Proclaim κηρύσσω
Prophet προφήτης –ου ὁ
Raise ἐγείρω
Read ἀναγινώσκω
Receive δέχομαι; λαμβάνω
Release ἀπολύω
Resurrection ἀνάστασις –εως ἡ
Righteous δίκαιος –α –ον
Righteousness δικαιοσύνη –ης ἡ
River πότεμος –ου ὁ
Run τρέχω
Sabbath σαββατον –ου τό
Saint See Holy
Salvation σωτηρία –ας ἡ
Same αὐτός –ή –ό
Save σῴζω
Say λέγω
Scribe γραμματεύς –έως ὁ
Scripture γραφή –ῆς ἡ
Sea θάλασσα –ης ἡ

See ὁράω
Send πέμπω
Servant δοῦλος –ου ὁ
She (See He)
Sick ἀσθενής –ές
Sin ἁμαρτία –ας ἡ
Sinner ἁμαρτωλός –οῦ ὁ
Slave See Servant
Small μικρός –α –ον
So that / in order that ἵνα
Soldier στρατιώτης –ου ὁ
Son υἱός –ου ὁ
Soul ψυχή –ῆς ἡ
Speak λέγω
Spirit πνεῦμα –ατος τό
Star ἀστήρ –έρος ὁ
Strong, be ἰσχύω
Synagogue συναγωγή –ῆς ἡ
Table τράπεζα –ῆς ἡ
Take λαμβάνω
Teach διδάσκω
Teacher διδάσκαλος –ου ὁ
Teaching διδασκαλία –ας ἡ
Temple ἱερόν –ου τό
Testify μαρτυρέω
There ἐκεῖ
These (See This)
They (See He)
Think νομίζω
Third τρίτος –η –ον
This οὗτος, αὕτη, τοῦτο
Through διά +gen
Throw βάλλω
To/Towards πρός, εἰς +acc
Tree δένδρον –ου τό
Trust n. πίστις –εως ἡ
Trust v. πιστεύω
Truth ἀλήθεια –ας ἡ

Appendix

Turn from ἀποστρέφω
United σύμφυτος –ον
Us (See We)
Voice φωνή –ης ἡ
Way ὁδός –ου ἡ
We (See I)
Who / Which / That ὅς, ἥ, ὅ
Wicked πονηρός –α –ον
Will (v) θέλω
Willing, be; (see Will)

Wish (See Will)
Word λόγος –ου ὁ
Work In ἐνεργέω
Work n. ἔργον –ου τό
World κόσμος –ου ὁ
Worship v.
Write γράφω
Year ἔτος –ους τό
You σύ

www.ingramcontent.com/pod-product-compliance
Lightning Source LLC
Chambersburg PA
CBHW070924160426
43193CB00011B/1576